# Contents

# Acknowledgements and References

I wish to thank Stirling University Computing Services, for word-processing advice and assistance; local schools, for completing questionnaires on pupil response to *Le Silence de la mer;* and my students, for their insights into an allegedly simple text whose simplicities continue to elude definition.

Page references **in bold type** are to the most recent (1986) edition of *'Le Silence de la mer' et autres récits,* Le Livre de Poche, no. 25 [Albin Michel, 1951], 190 pp., radically repaginated since the previous 251-page edition.

The title 'Le Silence de la mer' refers most infrequently to the definitive volume of stories. Contrary, therefore, to standard practice, it is *Le Silence de la mer* as individual story title, and the others, that have been italicised.

Abbreviations **in bold type** designate other Vercors works and a secondary source containing observations by the author which pre-date some of his autobiographical writings:

**BS**  *La Bataille du silence* (Presses de la Cité, 1967).

**H**  *Hamlet* (Éditions Vialetay, 1965), with 24 illustrations by Jean Bruller and preface by Vercors.

**MAB**  *Moi Aristide Briand, 1862-1932: Essai d'autoportrait. Cent Ans d'Histoire de France,* I (Plon, 1981).

**OP**  *L'Après-Briand (1932-1942): Les Occasions perdues, ou l'étrange déclin. Cent Ans d'Histoire de France,* II (Plon, 1982).

**NJ**  *Les Nouveaux Jours. Esquisse d'une Europe. Briand l'oublié (1942-1962). Cent Ans d'Histoire de France,* III (Plon, 1984).

**VED**  Radivoje D. Konstantinović, *Vercors Écrivain et Dessinateur* (Klincksieck, 1969).

Unless otherwise indicated, all sources cited are published in Paris. References to authors such as Flaubert will locate them in any edition. Notes, indicated by figures in superscript numbering to [38], are grouped together on pages 67-68.

# Introduction

Louis Aragon hailed it as a 'livre merveilleux de notre littérature' (**VED**, 9) Kléber Haedens dismissed it as a 'récit assez plat' whose success was 'entièrement inexpliqué'.[1] For Jacques Brenner, it was 'un événement dans la vie littéraire' which a history of 'literature' could legitimately ignore ('il est permis de ne pas le mentionner');[2] and Pierre Assouline was curiously backhanded: 'l'impact de ce livre publié sous le manteau ne sera pas seulement littéraire mais politique et moral'.[3] The work in question is of course *Le Silence de la mer*. First published under German occupation by the clandestine Éditions de Minuit in 1942, distributed illegally within France, parachuted back into it from London in 1943 where it was serialised in the Free French *La Marseillaise* and translated into English by Cyril Connolly in 1944, it took the engraver and illustrator Jean Bruller to international celebrity under the pseudonym Vercors. French Resistance historian Henri Michel wrote that 'par sa valeur littéraire et sa hauteur morale, il conférait une dimension nouvelle à la Résistance, sentie probablement à l'étranger encore plus qu'en France'.[4] The poet Lucien Scheler, Vercors's Resistance comrade in arms, suggests that 'dans une étude comparative des écrits de cette période tragique [...], l'historien des lettres françaises [...] devrait lui accorder une place aussi saisissante que celle que découvre le navigateur quand se présente à lui, à l'entrée du port de New-York, la statue de la Liberté'.[5] Fifty years after the events it describes, and despite the contemporary revisionism which much wartime writing has undergone, the story of the billeting of a cultured German officer in the home of a resolutely silent Frenchman and his niece remains almost iconic, a beacon, transcending history while remaining part of it:

> Parmi les livres nés de l'événement, un seul aura—et conservera—une profonde résonance: c'est *Le Silence de la mer*. Poignant et simple, ce récit est mieux qu'une œuvre de circonstances: la souffrance, non exprimée, rentrée, d'un impossible amour garde, aujourd'hui encore, sa puissance d'émotion.[6]

If its blend of didacticism and emotional poignancy have made *Le Silence de la mer* one of the most famous literary texts of the Second World War, it is also one of the most mythicised and most controversial, in part because of the circumstances of its publication and the mystery which surrounded the identity of its author until the Liberation. André Gide was one of a number of established writers suspected of producing a *récit* so obviously in the classic French tradition and which embodied 'universal' themes such as the obstacle to love and the conflict between private fulfilment and public duty; other candidates were Roger Martin du Gard, Marcel Arland,

Maurice Bedel, Jean Schlumberger (**BS**, 221) and Jacques de Lacretelle (**OP**, 244). Others still, notably the journalist Pascal Pia (**NJ**, 26-7) did not discourage the speculative attribution of the authorship of a work which was to prove fertile terrain for argument, even within the close-knit wartime group of Vercors's friends and colleagues such as Pierre de Lescure, co-founder of Les Éditions de Minuit, subsequently estranged. Pia later accused Vercors of having plagiarised an obscure German romance about the First World War (**NJ**, 133); more predictable analogies were drawn with Barrès's *Colette Baudoche*, though Vercors admitted only to having been influenced by a childhood memory of *Les Oberlé*, by René Bazin (**VED**, 65). The extent to which the writer was deemed to have forsaken his titular 'droits d'auteur' was further reflected in the pressure he came under from Jean-Pierre Melville and Jean Mercure, and to which against his better judgement he yielded, for the film and stage adaptations in 1948 and 1949.

More immediately damaging however than these 'menus épisodes de Landerneau-sur-Seine' (**NJ**, 27) was the fact that the volume, finely printed and bound by wartime standards and remarkably sympathetic in its portrayal of Werner von Ebrennac, divided Resistance members and sympathizers themselves. In a piece written from the embattled USSR, Ilya Ehrenbourg suggested that it might have emanated from the German propaganda machine (**NJ**, 41-2), an understandable speculation given the Nazi-inflicted horrors in the East but one not perhaps unconnected with a residual suspicion that the real author might yet turn out to be Gide, under Communist anathema since his prewar *Retour de l'URSS*. In the otherwise favourable political climate of wartime Britain, Arthur Koestler argued that even a German so imbued with Weimarian, pre-Hitlerian ideals as von Ebrennac could not have been ignorant of the true character of Nazism. More problematic was his critique of the French protagonists:

> The most exasperating thing in this booklet is its mixture of inferiority complex and arrogance. If ever there was a noble, well-meaning, unselfish friend of France, it is this wish-dream-hero von Ebrennac who carries his devotion to the point of suicide. Then why punish him with that stupid and arrogant silence? Only because this enlightened anti-Nazi was born of German parents? Here we have the uncannily precise repetition in 1942 of the mentality which in 1939 sent the German anti-Fascists in France to concentration camps. M. Vercors has learnt as little as the squabbling French politicians in exile.[7]

*Le Silence de la mer* was one of three works taken to task in 'The French Flu' (the others were Gide's *Interviews imaginaires* and Aragon's *Le Crève-Cœur*), but Koestler's facile analogy between the 'stupid and arrogant silence' of the French couple and the imprisonment of German exiles is doubly unjust. All states, rightly or wrongly, have practised the wartime detention of foreign nationals. In 1939, Britain interned German and Italian immigrants, some of them Jewish refugees from Nazism, some of them anti-fascist; and in the aftermath of the Nazi-Soviet pact (August 1939) and the banning of the French Communist Party (September) following its call for opposition to the 'imperialist' war, some German exiles in France (like their Spanish Republican counterparts) were rounded for their Communist sympathies as much as for their anti-Nazism, a fact which Koestler, still marked by his own internment at Le Vernet, disregards in his *ad hominem* attack on Vercors. None of which makes such policies morally more acceptable; the point is to underline how in the propaganda war which accompanied the military conflict, Vercors's *récit* quickly became part of more complex agendas. Koestler was on stronger ground in questioning the psychological verisimilitude of the couple's behaviour as distinct from its ideological desirability, and here his reference to 'a woolly, patriotic Franco-German allegory in terms of 1870 or rather even 1815' (*ibid.*) was echoed by no less a commentator than Sartre, who argued that the couple's silence revealed 'même un goût léger d'anachronisme: il rappelle le mutisme têtu des paysans patriotes de Maupassant pendant une autre occupation'.[8]

Von Ebrennac's credibility has continued to preoccupy historians. For Henri Michel, it was 'une gageure de faire parler, comme spécimen de l'occupant, un officier allemand cultivé, poli et, au fond de lui-même, francophile. Les internés de Fresnes, les hôtes de la rue des Saussaies [Gestapo headquarters in Paris], les condamnés au poteau du mont Valérien n'auraient certes pas reconnu en lui leurs ennemis, leurs tortionnaires souvent' (*Paris résistant*, p. 133). Gérard Loiseaux saw in him 'une hypothèse extrême de Vercors, qui a imaginé un officier de la Wehrmacht victime de la propagande nazie afin de démontrer que, *même avec un tel Allemand*, la collaboration était une duperie. Reste à savoir s'il y eut beaucoup de naïfs de ce genre dans les troupes d'occupation'.[9] Loiseaux does however argue that von Ebrennac 'par sa sincérité [...] devient malgré lui un médiateur fort convaincant. Il a toutes les chances, du moins jusqu'en fin 1942, de rendre la collaboration attirante pour les Français avec lesquels il engage le "dialogue"' (*ibid.*).

Part of the difficulty of the work's reception arose, as Loiseaux's additional qualification suggests, from the gap between the image of the German presented in the text and the reality inscribed in the evolution of events themselves. According to the author, *Le Silence de la mer* was composed between July and October 1941; the *achevé d'imprimer* celebrating 'ce volume publié aux dépens d'un patriote [...] sous l'occupation nazie' was dated 20 February 1942 (**BS**, 212).

Before it could be distributed to 350 pre-selected recipients, Lescure requested a delay for security reasons (**OP**, 243); one copy, given to Jean Paulhan and crudely duplicated, found its way from hand to hand, but the book did not circulate in the occupied zone in the numbers originally envisaged until October 1942 (**NJ**, 18). By then, Gestapo repression and the collusion between Vichy and the Germans had become much more apparent, with the executions of the 'groupe du Musée de l'Homme' (23 February)[10] and Jacques Decour (May), the imposition of the Yellow Star of David on Jews in the occupied zone and, in July, the infamous 'rafle du vel d'Hiv', the rounding up of men, women and children by the Paris police prior to deportation. It was only with the second printing, in July 1943, that the *récit* began to achieve the diffusion in France and overseas commensurate with its fast-growing reputation as an emblematic Resistance work. Vercors himself recalled that by 1944, 'moi-même [...] je ne pourrais plus écrire mon récit comme je l'ai fait trois ans plus tôt, du temps où l'occupant se voulait "correct", séducteur' (**NJ**, 42). And Sartre was undoubtedly right to argue that delay undercut the work's message, simply because as the mask of German correctness slipped, fewer people were likely to be taken in: 'une œuvre qui [...] eût présenté les soldats allemands en 41 comme des ogres eût fait rire et manqué son but. Dès la fin de 1942, *Le Silence de la mer* avait perdu son efficace' (*Qu'est-ce que la littérature?* p. 94). A more pertinent question for the contemporary scholar, however, is the extent to which, even in 1942, the story already presented an image of the Resistance which was essentially regressive and nostalgic.

Space, finally, as well as time was a factor, as Sartre reminded his postwar readers:

> Il est frappant que *Le Silence de la mer,* ouvrage qui fut écrit par un résistant de la première heure et dont le but est manifeste à nos yeux, n'ait rencontré que de l'hostilité dans les milieux émigrés de New York, de Londres, parfois même d'Alger et qu'on ait été jusqu'à taxer son auteur de collaborationnisme. C'est que Vercors ne visait pas *ce public-là.* Dans la zone occupée, au contraire, personne n'a douté des intentions de l'auteur ni de l'efficacité de son écrit: il écrivait pour nous. (*Qu'est-ce que la littérature?* pp. 92-3)

Sartre's explanation of the story's differential wartime impact—two publics, two perceptions—was a convincing, particular answer to a more general ideological problem. But even he forecast its inevitable eclipse—'dans un demi-siècle il ne passionnera plus personne; un public mal-renseigné le lira encore comme un conte agréable et un peu languissant sur la guerre de 1939' (*ibid.*, pp. 95-6), a prediction which some commentators may have hoped to see realized but which events have confounded. The 1970s and 1980s produced a historical, documentary and fictional flood of material on the French experience of the Second World War which shows no sign of abating and which has created a new readership for *Le Silence de la mer* in schools and universities. 1990 saw a 'reprise' of the stage version; new critical studies of the *récit* itself are in press, and as its half-century looms, it continues, transparently or enigmatically,[11] to occupy a unique position in the literary perception of the war years.

Integral to this process was the development of Vercors's career in works postdating *Le Silence de la mer* such as *Les Armes de la nuit* (1946), *Les Animaux dénaturés* (1952), and *Zoo* (1963), and the autobiographical *La Bataille du silence* (1967). The three-volume *Cent ans d'Histoire de France*, completed between 1981 and 1984, has added major dimensions, probably definitive, to the composite historico-biographical 'text' formed by the writer's life and writings, fictional and non-fictional. An invaluable account of Vercors's Resistance role and his contribution to Les Éditions de Minuit, these works offer remarkable insights on the conception and composition of the *récit*, many of whose central features were already in place before the historical catalyst of 1940. On the author's evidence, this was a text waiting to be written, a prophetic work imprinted with Vercors's uncanny ability to foresee events, and acquiring a different kind of intentionality from defeat.[12] Like the war itself, the origins of *Le Silence de la mer* lie in the 1930s; and like subsequent works, including the stage and film versions, its significance extends into the postwar period, when its ideological function was no longer to articulate the idea of resistance but to consecrate Vercors as 'Resistance Writer' and member, then President, of the Communist-dominated Comité National des Écrivains (CNE). That *Le Silence de la mer* has remained more widely read than his later writings is due in no small measure, as Margaret Atack has argued, to the fact that 'it functioned as a paradigm of the French (national) Resistance so enthusiastically espoused *after* the Liberation'.[13]

Alongside such a paradigmatic work, the 'other' stories Vercors wrote between 1943 and 1945, incorporated in the volume (1951) whose current derivative is the basis of the present study, have inevitably suffered by comparison. But though variable in quality and less original historically, some of them are interesting in their own right, as examples of Resistance writing and as reflections of a certain wartime experience. The 'documentary' qualities ascribed to *Le Silence de la mer* by Roderick Kedward[14] are characteristic also of *Désespoir est mort* (1943) and *L'Imprimerie de Verdun* (1945). *La Marche à l'étoile* (1943) shows how Republican, democratic values succumbed to the totalitarianism of 'le port de l'étoile', a lasting emblem of man's inhumanity to man and a theme further explored in 1944 in 'la nouvelle pleine de rage que j'appellerai *L'Impuissance*' (**NJ**, 45). *Ce Jour-là* is a neat cameo of danger and resistance seen through a child's eyes in which the mysterious removal of a 'pot de géranium' from the window (an agreed but unexpected signal between the parents), the child's ignorance of what is happening, the solitude of the father, the enigmatic remarks of the grown-ups— 'oui, lui aussi [...] il cherchait à apercevoir sa femme dans un compartiment, ils l'ont reconnu' (**90**)—are more compelling for being allusive and understated. This contrasts strikingly with *Le Cheval et la mort* (1944) in which an elderly Parisian caretaker is faced with the vision of Hitler, '"aussi horrifique et redoutable que si c'eût été la Mort, la Mort avec sa faux et son linceul et ce sourire sinistre dans les mâchoires sans lèvres"' (**107**). The hallucinatory quality reappears in the image of the grotesque, mutilated companion who leads the narrrator of *Le Songe* through unnatural visions of death and decay, of dark deeds evocative of Bosch, Daumier and Goya, until a recognition occurs: 'Je revois mon compagnon à la langue brûlée. Sa face carrée, blanche, torturée et qui m'offre toujours ce sourire secret et glacé—et je comprends bien maintenant que c'était le sourire de Yorick' (**83**).

   *Le Songe* was inspired by the experiences of Jacques Chardonne's son, Gérard Boutelleau, in Oranienburg concentration camp in 1943, *L'Impuissance* was written in response to the death of the critic Benjamin Crémieux in Buchenwald in 1944. But if circumstance played a part in these and other stories, as did the need to provide 'copy' for the clandestine reviews in which they appeared, it would be unwise to suggest as Konstantinović does that the only link between some of them is provided by events (**VED**, 176). This is partly because they share a number of thematic and stylistic features, including cultural references which function both as narrative and ideological codes, and because, as Jean Attali reminds us, 'la logique de l'œuvre et celle des événements' are not coterminous, 'si réels qu'en soient les effets'.[15] Though it may have a basis in reality, 'l'œuvre s'impose dans son époque par son rythme, son avance ou son retard, c'est-à-dire, tout ensemble par sa prophétie et son *hystérésis*. [...] Dans son progrès, à travers inventions et ruptures, elle finit par produire sa propre structure réflexive' (*ibid.*).

   At its most basic, this disjuncture, this 'project', is expressed in the difference between the order in which the stories were composed, and the order in which the book offers them to be read. *Désespoir est mort*, despite its introductory position in the volume, was written after *Le Silence de la mer* and arguably because the latter had been written. The closing piece, *La Marche à l'étoile*, published in 1943 in memory of Vercors's father and against the anti-Semitism to which he would have fallen victim had he lived until the Occupation, appears to echo stories which in fact it preceded. The narrator of *Le Songe* evokes his initial reluctance to identify with the victims' suffering—'Le parfum de votre chocolat, le matin, le goût du croissant frais, comme ils avaient plus de présence...' (**74**)—in terms which recall one of Jean Bruller's drawings of the 1930s.

Similar complexities arise at the interface between the fictional and the autobiographical works. Consider for example the powerful maritime metaphor which illuminates the title of the *récit:* 'sous la calme surface des eaux, la mêlée des bêtes dans la mer, [...] la vie sous-marine des sentiments cachés, des désirs et des pensées qui se nient et qui luttent' (**55**). In 1967, Vercors claimed to have added these lines to the manuscript by way of afterthought and in response to the perplexity of his printer (**BS**, 203). If so, the afterthought was inspired, since the metaphor simultaneously suggests the apparent implacability of the French couple's resistance—silent, natural, forceful; the contrast represented in von Ebrennac between the surface of German civilisation and the underlying monstrosity of Nazism; and, finally, the character's own unspoken, perhaps unconscious, conflicts. Yet *Le Songe* likens the corpse of a concentration camp inmate to 'une méduse échouée sur le sable' (**81**); and the narrator's comment that 'ce fut un peu comme si j'étais regardé par une bête sous-marine, comme par un poulpe' (**82**) suggests that such imagery and the association thereby created between 'la mort' and 'la mer', subtly developed in the evocation of 'le visage que la mort avait nettoyé de ses impuretés' (**81**), were more central to his artistic and imaginative vision than he was aware at the time or subsequently willing to admit.

The likelihood that psycho-affective forces underlie these images, and the extent to which autobiographical works in which we seek illumination on Vercors-as-writer necessarily tell us much about Vercors-as-reader of himself, are significantly reinforced by the *autoportrait* of Briand which he published in 1981. Explaining his imaginative identification with the statesman whose 'naissance au Parlement' coincided with his own birth in 1902, and whose policy of Franco-German reconciliation determined his own political creed in the 1920s and 1930s, he revealed 'une vieille tendresse coupable' (**MAB**, 9), a long-standing ambivalence already expressed indirectly in von Ebrennac. Further exploration of Briand's past in *Les Occasions perdues* produced a more striking revelation, 'un curieux phénomène de mémoire':

> Sous chaque pierre que je soulevais dans les eaux du passé historique je découvrais, tapi comme un 'dormeur', un morceau oublié du mien. Sans le vouloir, je ramenais ainsi l'un après l'autre à la surface, mêlés aux événements, mes souvenirs personnels engloutis. (**OP**, 7)

The involuntary ('sans le vouloir') nature of 'ce temps retrouvé surgi du fond des mers' casts further doubt on the gratuitousness of the previously-quoted passage in *Le Silence de la mer*, and suggests that what is remembered by Bruller/Briand is remembered because Bruller became Vercors/von Ebrennac, and belongs as much to the text since written as to the 'pre-text'. This does not necessarily make all such information untrue, and in dealing with works whose ostensible purpose was didactic, it is scarcely possible to exclude all reference to authorial intention and perception, however 'fallacious'; but it reminds us when in doubt to cleave to the Lawrentian dictum of trusting the tale, not the teller.

The present study concentrates on *Le Silence de la mer*, and devotes a chapter to *Désespoir est mort*, *L'Imprimerie de Verdun* and *L'Impuissance*, which merit consideration for their historico-documentary dimensions and as part of Vercors's critique of political attitudes through narrative and characterisation. Reference to other stories will in the main be for corroboration or illustration only; opinions will doubtless differ on the value-judgment implied in this selection. By way of contextualisation for the reader unfamiliar with the period, France's place in the 'New European Order', the political and moral problematics of collaborationism, and Vercors's role in the events of the period are examined. The structure of the study, which begins with a brief biography of Vercors (Jean Bruller) until the fall of France in the summer of 1940, is broadly chronological, the critical perspective bifocal — literature is part of history and transcends history — the methodology undogmatic. 'Transgressive' interpretations are not ignored — how could they be, in respect of a work whose capacity to mythicise the Occupation simultaneously articulates and undercuts its didactic (anti-German) message? But we do well to remember in our contemporary 'Ère du soupçon' and in a Europe at peace with itself if not the rest of the world for half a century, that writing about *Le Silence de la mer* is a reassuringly safe activity compared to the dangers Vercors ran to write and publish it.

# Chapter One

## From Jean Bruller to Vercors

**Portrait of the artist**

Jean Marcel Bruller was born in Paris on 26 February 1902, second child of Ernestine Bourbon and Louis Bruller. His mother was a *Berrichonne* whose maiden name enabled her son humorously to claim royal antecedents (**OP**, 23-4), and provided the thinly-disguised variant 'Chambord' in *La Marche à l'étoile* (**167**). His father was a Hungarian of Jewish extraction whose family had originally emigrated eastwards from the Vosges—the name Bruller is Alsatian—and who at the age of fifteen, penniless, idealistic, and a victim of the anti-Semitism of Austria-Hungary's second city, had set out on foot from Budapest 'par amour de Hugo, de la Liberté, de l'Égalité et de la nouvelle de Hauff: *l'Orpheline du Pont des Arts*' (**OP**, 249-50). Upon arrival in Paris and before seeking a bed for the night, he went first to see the cityscape from the Pont des Arts. There, by one of the coincidences characteristic of Vercors's own life, he had a chance meeting with another Hungarian, thanks to whom he became a successful popular publisher of Hugo and Eugène Sue. Some of these details were recounted to Vercors by an elderly Jewess he met in Marseilles in 1942, many years after his father's death in 1930, and the reality may have been more prosaic, but there can be no doubting Bruller senior's long-standing admiration for things French, and its place in the 'family history' of the author.

Jean Bruller's early years were spent in comfortable circumstances in Paris with his parents and an older sister. He later recalled the security of his childhood in the flat in the rue Charles Divry behind the *mairie* of the fourteenth arrondissement (**OP**, 89-90); his father subsequently acquired a new apartment block in the same district, in a street situated between the present-day Avenue René Coty and the Rue du Saint-Gothard which now bears his name (**NJ**, 321-2). In 1909 the family visited Hungary, where Jean met an uncle who held an important position at the Imperial court and from whose lips, apparently, he first heard the talismanic name 'BRRIAND' (**MAB**, 10). Like other 'sensations indélébiles de l'enfance' (**OP**, 90), the impressions of this journey he took at the age of seven were to remain printed on his visual and affective memory—'une telle vision ne s'oublie pas' (**NJ**, 369)—and perhaps helped to develop a sense of the exotic-in-the-familiar which is one of the characteristics of his pictorial work. Like André Gide before him, he attended the École Alsacienne (the male line in his father's family was Protestant), but he seems to have grown up in a non-religious domestic environment; he later called himself 'incroyant de naissance' (**OP**, 26) and 'résolument [...] rationaliste' (**NJ**, 22). He took his *baccalauréat* at the end of the First World War, and as a student engineer at the École d'Électricité Bréguet, was involved as a strike-breaker in the tram workers' dispute of 1921, evincing a political and social naïveté which he subsequently attributed to his 'enfance prolongée' (**OP**, 8). His stated literary tastes were unexceptional for his age group and milieu, though retrospection may have given the succession of authors read—Anatole France at sixteen, Gide at twenty, Proust at twenty-five (**NJ**, 116)—a greater degree of deliberation than was the case. In 1924, a 'sous-lieutenant de réserve tout frais promu' (*ibid.*, 251), Bruller fulfilled six months' national service in the North African colony of Tunisia, and upon return to civilian life embarked upon a career as artist and engraver which lasted until the outbreak of another war with Germany in 1939.

His first two albums of cartoons, the macabrely-entitled *21 Recettes pratiques de mort violente* (1924) and *Hypothèses sur les amateurs de la peinture* (1926) were an immediate success. He contributed pieces to journals and by 1930 had established himself as an illustrator of distinction in works by Kipling, Maurois and Poe. His abiding fascination with Shakespeare dated from the late 1920s, though it was not until the 1940s that he began to realize his 'rêve le plus cher, [...] illustrer *Hamlet* d'eaux-fortes' (**NJ**, 11). *Un Homme coupé en tranches* (1929) was followed in 1932 by the first 'relevés trimestriels', subsequently incorporated in *La Danse des vivants* (1938). These woodcuts, like *Visions intimes et rassurantes de la guerre* (1932-1938), gave a topical flavour to perennial problems: the piece entitled 'massacres, pestes et famines' portrays the smug complacency of the bourgeois abed with newspaper, coffee and croissants, reading about contemporary catastrophes. *La Nouvelle Clé des songes* and *Folies douces* displayed a familiarity with darker, irrational dimensions of human behaviour and the interpretation of dreams, about which Bruller consulted the psychoanalyst Rudolph Loewenstein (**OP**, 7-8), and lent support to his claim that his muse was 'intemporelle' (*ibid.,* 89).

Konstantinović is unduly schematic in arguing that 'il est indispensable de connaître le pessimisme fondamental de Jean Bruller dessinateur, pour bien comprendre la recherche obstiné de l'espérance humaine qui caractérisera ensuite les écrits de Vercors' (**VED**, 6). But the sombre nature of much of the pre-war artwork, its blend of violence and detached indifference, is consistent with the writer's own, retrospective evocation of a man divided, 'constamment partagé en deux moitiés antagonistes' (**OP**, 26). On the one hand, he experienced a profound sense of the futility of attempting to influence events:

> Incroyant de naissance, je ne peux [..] me résoudre à supposer un sens à l'Univers, encore moins à l'espèce humaine. Ainsi le bien, le mal, la paix, la guerre, le socialisme, le fascisme, agitation insensée d'insectes. Par conséquent, se garder de cette agitation et, première règle, éviter de souffrir, la souffrance étant d'évidence, au sein d'une existence 'absurde', la pire des absurdités. (*ibid.*)

This pessimistic view of human activity—'agitation insensée d'insectes'—and the almost Pascalian quietism advanced as an existential rule, conflicted however with a contrary impulse, the powerful, visceral lure of action—'je ne peux m'empêcher d'agir' (*ibid.*)—and the intellectual necessity for a self-confessed humanist to behave in conformity with his values and beliefs.

As one whose adolescence was marked by wartime and by stories of Verdun (1916) told by his future brother-in-law Pierre Fort, a lieutenant in the French army, the young Bruller professed an understandable 'haine du "Boche"' (**OP**, 9). By temperament and conviction, however, he was drawn increasingly to non-violence, and after the failure of France's attempt to exact reparations by occupying the Ruhr in 1923, was converted to the policy of Franco-German reconciliation pursued by Briand and the Weimar Republic's foreign minister, Gustave Stresemann. This policy proved difficult to maintain after the latter's death in 1929 and the onset of the Great Depression which hit France in 1932, the year in which Briand himself died. His centre-right and Radical successors such as Tardieu, Laval, Herriot and Daladier were 'mous' (**OP**, 58; 62), 'faux-durs' (**NJ**, 10), unwilling either to work energetically for peace or to strengthen France's defences against resurgent German militarism. Such judgements bear the wisdom of hindsight, but the writer's admitted reluctance to oppose the reoccupation of the Rhineland in 1936 (**OP**, 105) gives them a considerable degree of validity for his attitudes at the time.

In 1935, an invitation to contribute a weekly political cartoon to the anti-fascist newspaper *Vendredi*, edited by the writers André Chamson, Andrée Viollis, Jean Guéhenno and Louis Martin-Chauffier, associated Bruller with the Popular Front, which came to power under Léon Blum in 1936. He also enjoyed the friendship of Jules Romains, author of *Les Hommes de bonne volonté* and secretary of the French section of the PEN-Club which played a prominent role in organising intellectuals and artists in the political debates of the interwar years. Discussions with Romains, whom he accompanied on a visit to Prague in the summer of 1938, and with the Communist Jean-Richard Bloch, helped to shape his views on communism and pacifism, ideologies which continued to exercise a powerful hold over important sections of the left and centre-left.

Politics also brought Bruller into contact with other 'committed' intellectuals of the period, including Aragon, Drieu la Rochelle and Ramon Fernandez. The impression of reserve which emerges from his later works may derive partly from knowledge of what some of them (such as the fellow-traveller-turned-collaborator Fernandez) subsequently became (**OP**, 90). But he seems also to have been ambivalent about the highly public position-taking of an age of manifestos and counter-manifestos, declarations and apologias, of which Roger Martin du Gard complained that most might have been entitled 'moi et la révolution'[16] He recalled the 'passionnantes' editorial discussions at *Vendredi,* which he attended as a 'témoin le plus souvent muet' (*ibid.*); admiring Chamson's verbal facility at a public homage to Romain Rolland, he confessed that '[je] préférais mourir que de prendre la parole' (**OP**, 118).

A close friend and, given Bruller's political sympathies, perhaps a surprising one, was Diego Brosset, son-in-law of the First-World-War General Mangin; at his home Bruller met Maxime Weygand, the Commander-in-chief who was to preside over France's defeat in June 1940 and in whose vigorous right-wing views he sensed trouble ahead for the Republic (*ibid.*, 91). Brosset had a property at Irus in the Gulf of Morbihan, 'une espèce d'île déserte' (**NJ**, 32), where they indulged a common passion for sailing (Bruller was also an enthusiastic skier). In 1931, Bruller married Jeanne Barussaud; twin boys were born in 1934, and the family home at Villiers-sur-Morin near Meaux in the Marne valley also provided a refuge in troubled times. He was skiing at Montana when the riots of 6 February 1934 provoked a major political crisis; and sailing in Brittany during the build-up of international tension in September 1938. This ability periodically to distance himself from events while remaining aware of their looming presence and evolution seems to have amounted to a form of premonitory sixth sense. An engraving executed in 1935 predicted the German breakthrough in Northern France, 'à une semaine près, à Bapaume, le 12 mai 1940' (**BS**, 17). As he crossed Germany on his return from Prague in 1938, the visible preparations for war filled him with a foreboding not dispelled by the Munich settlement. To his mother's 'mes enfants, nous sommes sauvés!' he replied: 'mais dans un an nous serons tous vassalisés' (**OP**, 152). His prescience was shortly to be tested.

Aged thirty-seven, and retaining his reserve rank of lieutenant, Bruller was mobilised in September 1939. He was based first at Embrun in the south-eastern Alps, and then near Romans on the river Isère, where he saw and admired the mountain massif whose name he was to adopt for his creative pseudonym. In November, during the *drôle de guerre,* he was sent to the north-western sector

near Reims; a broken leg and the very inexpert treatment he received
caused him to limp for some time thereafter. On his recovery, he
requested transfer to 'la topographie divisionnaire [...] où l'on
s'expose au front avec la troupe, sans mettre personne en danger'
(**OP**, 182) but this attempt to use his draughtsman's skills and
reconcile honour with non-violence proved fruitless. He rejoined his
unit at the end of March, once again in the south-east; he was there
when the German offensive in the west began on 10 May 1940, and
when hostilities ended six weeks later with the most comprehensive
military defeat in France's history.

Prime Minister Reynaud and some of his cabinet had wished to
fight on from Brittany or North Africa, but Weygand and Marshal
Philippe Pétain, the eighty-four-year-old 'vainqueur de Verdun'
brought into the government as deputy Premier to bolster civilian
and military morale, were convinced that an accommodation must be
sought with the enemy. The armistice signed at Rethondes on 22 June
1940 disbanded the army and air force, divided France into occupied
and unoccupied zones, and imposed daily costs of four hundred
million francs. Hostilities with Italy, which had declared war on 10
June, were ended by a separate agreement. It was a profound
humiliation, even to many of those who greeted the end of hostilities
with relief. A minority had already taken steps to continue the fight:
de Gaulle's 'appel du 18 juin' 1940, issued over the BBC from
London, marked the beginning of the Free French Resistance. To
most observers, however, he was an isolated, dissident and unknown
figure, and Britain's own defeat seemed merely a matter of time.
France's military losses of 92,000 were four times the German
figure; over one and a half million of her troops were taken
prisoner.

In the universal calamity, to have fought and lost was perhaps
only exceeded in its futility by not having fought at all, but Bruller's
residual commitment to non-violence makes that conjectural.
*Désespoir est mort,* based on the author's experiences in June 1940,
evokes powerful feelings of shame and disgust, but was written some
two and half years after the events and has an artistic necessity
relating to a later period. According to *La Bataille du silence,* he
briefly contemplated joining de Gaulle but was deflected from this
course by military-bureaucratic ineptitude. He sought the approval of
his colonel (!), who sought clearance from Division (!), which not
unnaturally refused; as the Germans advanced south of Lyon, a
departure 'quand même' would have smacked of desertion in the face
of the enemy (**BS**, 76-7). The mock rearguard action, 'la bataille
postiche' which Bruller's unit was asked to mount between the
signature of the armistice and the ending of hostilities (25 June), was
the occasion of a revelation: 'je découvris que, dans l'action, je

n'étais pas un chef, mais un intellectuel radoteur. Je me rappelais Hamlet, hésitant si le spectre qu'il avait vu était bien son père ou le diable' (*ibid.*, 62). Despite its literariness, this expression of visceral indecision is consistent with other manifestations of Bruller's contrary dispositions: the conflict between self-effacing introspection and the desire for action and participation, the curious psycho-imaginative *dédoublement* whereby 'on est souvent son propre spectateur'(*ibid.*, 113).

Rationalised after the event, these episodes became part of the 'étrange chapelet des hasards qui m'avaient retenu à Romans sans même me permettre de tirer un seul coup de fusil' (*ibid.*) and which, by preventing Bruller being taken prisoner or joining de Gaulle, led indirectly to the composition of *Le Silence de la mer*. Nationally the times may have been 'out of joint' in 1940, but in personal terms they were auspicious for the 'birth' of Vercors, the artist-turned-writer propelled to the forefront of events by forces greater than himself, and to celebrity 'malgré lui'.

## Collaboration and Resistance: the role of the writer

On 10 July 1940 at Vichy, administrative and political 'capital' of the unoccupied zone, the assembled Deputies and Senators voted the abolition of the Third Republic. It was replaced by the authoritarian 'État Français' of Pétain and Laval, who promised a return to the 'traditional' values embodied in the slogan *Travail, Famille, Patrie*. To a defeated and demoralised nation, some ten million of whom had been scattered by the exodus and faced the yawning gap revealed between illusion and reality—French propaganda posters had claimed in 1940 that 'nous vaincrons parce que nous sommes les plus forts'—, this programme seemed to offer a return to normality and, in its apparent willingness to tackle long-standing demographic and economic problems, a prospect of renewal. By denouncing the tyranny of capital as well as organised labour, and by giving a ministerial post to the former trades union leader René Belin, Pétain also seemed to acknowledge the nation's aspirations towards social justice. His offer of the 'don de ma personne' to the country in its hour of need,[17] his expressed 'hatred' for 'les mensonges qui vous ont fait tant de mal' (*ibid.*, p. 25), his serene assurance that he would keep the promises made to the nation, 'même celles des autres', all struck a chord. In addition, his personal prestige, charisma and age were considered auguries of sagacity and guarantees against dangerous political adventurism.

But to those familiar with the extreme right-wing ideas of Charles Maurras, whose hatred of the Republic produced undisguised

satisfaction in defeat, some of Pétain's statements struck a disquieting
note. On 15 August 1940, he affirmed that 'Il n'y a pas de neutralité
possible entre le vrai et le faux, entre le bien et le mal, entre la santé
et la maladie, entre l'ordre et le désordre, entre la France et l'Anti-
France' (*ibid.*, p. 47). Vichy was no sooner in place than the first
repressive legislation was introduced; repression extended not simply
to the Communists, already excluded from the political community
since September 1939, but to Socialists of most hues, to Jews (both
categories conveniently united in Blum), and to other enemies of the
régime such as Radicals and Freemasons. The myth of the military,
industrial and social damage caused by the hated Popular Front led to
the creation of a special Supreme Court at Riom to try those held
responsible for the defeat. Since Vichy was tapping into an
indigenous tradition of intolerance stretching back to the Dreyfus
affair (1894) and beyond (Drumont, Gobineau), these measures
required no prompting from the invader; but they received
additional ideological endorsement from Pétain's meeting with Hitler
at Montoire on 24 October 1940, of which he declared: 'C'est dans
l'honneur et pour maintenir l'unité française [...] dans le cadre d'une
activité constructive du nouvel ordre européen, que j'entre
aujourd'hui dans la voie de la collaboration' (*ibid.*, p. 88).

The history of the next four years is in part the story of how
Vichy's 'Collaboration d'État' increasingly coincided with the
ideological collaborationism preached in occupied Paris by fascist
intellectuals and party leaders such as Drieu la Rochelle, Robert
Brasillach, Jacques Doriot and Marcel Déat, for whom the thousand-
year Reich and France's place in the 'New Europe' had considerable
seductive power. The collapse of the Republic, the apparently
effortless superiority of the Germans, and their generally 'correct'
behaviour towards the civilian population were exploited by the
occupying authorities and their French apologists. There were of
course exceptions: Jean Moulin, in 1940 Prefect of the Eure and
subsequently De Gaulle's emissary to the internal Resistance,
witnessed German atrocities at Chartres; the poet Saint-Pol-Roux, to
whom *Le Silence de la mer* was dedicated, was brutally beaten at
Camaret (he later died), his daughter raped and his elderly servant
killed. But the contrast between the behaviour the French had been
led to expect and the conduct of most of the occupying forces was
perceptible to all but the most partisan observers. The poster entitled
'Populations abandonnées, faites confiance au soldat allemand', which
portrayed an unhelmeted German soldier holding a French child in
his arms, was an obvious propaganda ploy and yet consistent with the
author's own experience at Saintes where he had joined his family
following demobilisation at the end of July 1940:

> Les Allemands se sont bien conduits, partout. Ni violences ni pillages.
> Au contraire: aimables, empressés, payant rubis sur l'ongle, attentifs et
> câlins avec les enfants, charitables avec les réfugiés que parfois même
> ils aident à se loger, à transporter des meubles. Les Juifs, les
> Communistes? Question jamais posée. C'était cela, ces hommes
> abominables? Ces brutes? ces tortionnaires? Propagande! On nous a
> trompés. (**BS**, 111)

The week spent in the Charente was also the occasion of a more
extended reminiscence, still vivid in the writer's memory some thirty
years later:

> Depuis huit jours je suis au milieu des miens, dans le calme estival de
> Montcharente, belle maison sur le coteau que parfume un magnolia
> géant, toujours en fleur. La vue sur la vallée, où la rivière serpente dans
> les prairies, fait verdoyer le cœur. Mon Dieu, mon Dieu, la vie est là,
> simple et tranquille...
> [...] A Saintes, me dit ma mère, la population avait fait aux vainqueurs
> un accueil chaleureux, les filles agitant des mouchoirs, des écharpes
> pour ces jeunes motards athlétiques, beau comme des dieux et qui les
> regardaient en riant. Ah! dans une autre guerre, qu'il eût été apaisant de
> pouvoir me réjouir de cette concorde, de pouvoir croire à cette
> réconciliation! Hélas! dans cette attitude des Français, je ne pouvais
> trouver que lâcheté ou aveuglement, sans même savoir ce qui serait le
> pire. Des lâches, la première peur passée, peuvent se reprendre, se
> réveiller. Des aveugles risquent de n'ouvrir les yeux que lorsqu'il sera
> trop tard. (*ibid.*, 111-12)

This passage contains thematic, stylistic and ideological material
characteristic of *Le Silence de la mer:* the writer's dismay at the
attitude of the population, interested in material questions and the
beauty of the 'jeunes motards athlétiques'; his nostalgia for
reconciliation—if only it had been 'l'autre guerre'; the suggestion of
'permanence' conveyed by the 'toujours en fleur', redolent of an
unchanging provincial reality; and the central distinction between the
dangerous (because likely to remain permanent) blindness of some,
and the damaging (but possibly temporary) cowardice of others who
might be saved for the fight.

No such distinction seemed possible however between the merely
'lâches' or 'aveugles' and those whose lucid espousal of
collaborationism was to prove one of the stigmata of the age. Among
the first of these were writers Bruller had previously admired, such
as Jacques Lenormand, Luc Durtain, and Jacques Chardonne, whose
'L'Été à la Maurie' drew a very different conclusion from the
invader's arrival in the Charente.[18] The reappearance of the
prestigious *Nouvelle Revue Française* under the 'new' management
of Drieu la Rochelle, the censorship of all printed material, the 'liste
Otto' of books, authors and publishers banned by the occupier, the
control which could be exercised over an already docile press by the
rationing of supplies of newsprint, all showed that intellectual

conformity would be an integral part of the 'new order'.

Collaborationism posed the question of the writer's duty and raised the spectre of a 'trahison des clercs' more serious than that described by Julien Benda in his work of that name in 1927. Georges Politzer was unambiguous: 'Aujourd'hui, en France, littérature légale veut dire: littérature de trahison'.[19] Recalling 'l'épouvantable défection d'écrivains auxquels certaines réussites formelles avaient donné à l'étranger une manière de gloire', Jean-Richard Bloch wrote:

> Un Maurras, un Giono, un Montherlant, un Paul Morand, un Céline [...] ont joué, vis-à-vis de notre pays, le rôle de ces pierres dont les auteurs d'un drame crapuleux alourdissent les poches de leur victime pour être sûrs qu'elle ira au fond et ne remontera jamais à la surface.[20]

Bruller, like Jean Guéhenno and others, decided not to publish under the German *imprimatur* and withdrew to Villiers. Here he worked for the local joiner, a physical and spiritual retreat understandable in the circumstances and probably therapeutic: practical manual work would be a distraction from the inadequacy, real or perceived, of artistic and intellectual endeavour, pending auguries of renewal. For the foreseeable future, there could be but 'un seul devoir, [...] une seule loi: se taire' (**BS**, 137).

The road from 'se taire' to 's'exprimer', from quiescent 'silence du mépris'[21] to voiced resistance, needs only brief recall here. Contrary to expectation, Britain was not defeated; some colonies rallied to de Gaulle; the first clandestine publications, including *Pantagruel* (October 1940) and *Résistance* (December), together with acts of defiance such as the student demonstration at the Arc de Triomphe on 11 November, created awareness of a will to resist, as yet inchoate and unstructured but already dangerous. The young engineer Jacques Bonsergent was shot on Christmas Eve 1940; Bruller, who with Pierre Dalloz and Pierre de Lescure, had helped to establish an escape network for allied airmen, saw the posters announcing the execution on the streets of Paris (**BS**, 151). Thanks to Lescure he became involved in the clandestine journal *La Pensée libre*, committed to fighting the invader but too exclusively Communist in tenor, and likely therefore to confirm the German propaganda claim that their opponents were mostly Communists and Jews. The same propaganda presented German economic exploitation of France as a partnership, the invasion of the USSR on 22 June 1941 as a crusade for Western civilisation (Christendom, Charlemagne) against Judeo-Bolshevik barbarism, and justified the execution of civilian hostages as a legitimate military response to Resistance 'terrorism'. It was in order to broaden the range of contributions to *La Pensée libre*, and thus enhance its political effectiveness, that

Bruller embarked upon the story which subsequently became *Le
Silence de la mer*. When the journal foundered with the capture of its
principal organizers, he and Lescure resolved to pursue the task in a
different way. For the characteristic of 'une pensée libre', as Vercors
argued in a speech delivered in April 1945, is its refusal to be
defined, in specificity or intensity, by the force to which it is
opposed.[22] He drew a distinction between what he called 'actes de la
pensée', essentially circumstantial works produced in response to
events, and those 'œuvres de "pensée sereine"' (*ibid,* pp. 15-16)
which might fulfil an important didactic purpose—to bear witness to
the permanence, the beauty, the *mesure* of the French
spirit—precisely because they did not subscribe to purely
oppositional values:

> Des journaux clandestins, depuis *Pantagruel* il en naît chaque semaine
> (et il en disparaît autant ou presque). Plus 'anti-Boches' qu'antinazis,
> plus soucieux d'inspirer la haine que la justice, leur fougue guerrière et
> sanglante est sûrement nécessaire pour stimuler la combativité des
> militants. Je les admire et je les approuve. Toutefois ma vocation, à moi,
> est différente. Elle est, au sein de l'action violente—de ses vicissitudes,
> parfois de ses erreurs—, de permettre à des esprits exacts de publier
> sous le manteau des réflexions exactes, méditées dans la rigueur, non
> moins sévères d'ailleurs pour l'ennemi et même d'autant plus sévères
> qu'elles sont en marge de la colère, de la passion—en un mot de
> permettre à ces esprits fidèles à la longue tradition française, de penser
> juste. (**OP**, 230-1)

*Le Silence de la mer* would unmask collaborationism, not by
portraying a direct confrontation between the occupying forces and
French Resistance fighters, still few in number in 1941, but by
making a cultured and civilised German officer the dupe of his own
propaganda. And by having the manuscript properly printed and
carefully bound, Vercors ensured that its ideological message would
be replicated in its physical form. These tasks were accomplished in
conditions of secrecy and at considerable personal risk to those
involved, whence the resonantly 'nocturnal'' title chosen for the
underground publishing venture with which *Le Silence de la mer*
came into being.

# Chapter Two

## *Le Silence de la mer*

### The story and the stories

The action opens with von Ebrennac being billeted in the French couple's home in November 1940, a date noticeably posterior to the armistice, and covers a period of some seven months until his departure the following July. The couple, described by their uninvited guest as 'un vieil homme digne. Et une demoiselle silencieuse' (**32-3**), decide to ignore him: 'de ne rien changer à notre vie, fût-ce le moindre détail: comme si l'officier n'existait pas; comme s'il eût été un fantôme' (**25**). He accepts their silence as a challenge and embarks on an account of his vision of a new future for France and Germany, united in a European 'marriage'. Cultured and sensitive, a musician in civilian life, much travelled (though not before to France), endowed with enough French to hold forth fluently on his subject, though probably unversed in conversational niceties that are not required, von Ebrennac never departs from his 'correct' demeanour. He compliments the couple on their patriotism and on the spiritual qualities of their home—'j'éprouve un grand estime pour les gens qui aiment leur patrie' (**23**); 'cette maison a une âme' (**31**)—and expresses the desire to be accepted 'comme le fils d'un village pareil' (**37**).

His Francophilia is not entirely uncritical, however. He recalls his late father's hopes of international reconciliation, hopes which foundered on the opposition of the French, of their 'grands bourgeois cruels' such as the industrial magnate de Wendel or 'votre vieux Maréchal' (**28**), presumably a reference not to Pétain but to Foch, who died in 1929. He contrasts the couple's uncompromising stance with the compliant attitude encountered by his troops on their entry to Saintes in the summer of 1940: '"J'étais heureux que la population nous recevait bien. [...] Et puis, j'ai vu [...] que c'était la lâcheté. [...] J'ai méprisé ces gens"' (**32**). He is equally contemptuous of prominent collaborators such as Admiral Darlan, Prime Minister from February 1941 until April 1942: 'un chef qui n'a pas l'amour des siens est un bien misérable mannequin. [...] Qui donc, sinon un aussi morne ambitieux, eût accepté ce rôle?' (**43**). His hosts find it increasingly difficult to resist his sincerity and, in the niece's case, the unstated appeal of a courtship conducted through fable (Beauty and the Beast) and music; the room contains a harmonium on which von Ebrennac plays a Bach prelude abandoned by the girl since the invasion. Pursued 'pendant plus de cent soirées d'hiver' (**38**), his 'interminable monologue' is unfailingly closed with 'je vous souhaite une bonne nuit', which, like his limping tread on the stairs, punctuates the story.

A meeting in Paris with those responsible for implementing the collaboration leads to sudden disillusionment: far from a partnership, collaboration is a lure—'nous les bernons [.] *Wir prellen sie'* (**53**)—to reduce France to servitude and intellectual barrenness, to make her 'une chienne rampante' (*ibid.*). Far from ascending to the sunlit uplands of personal and national fulfilment, German policy will lead down towards 'une vallée sinistre, [...] dans les ténèbres fétides d'une lugubre forêt' (**58**), to a dark and squalid corruption. The reality of Nazi barbarism is made clear: the books will be banned or burnt, 'pas seulement vos Péguy, vos Proust, vos Bergson... Mais tous les autres!' (**55**). The examples are telling ones, both by their historical-documentary appropriateness and their wider symbolism: Péguy, the Catholic poet killed in the previous war and associated with Chartres, one of the stages on von Ebrennac's invasion route; the philosopher Bergson, a Jewish convert to Christianity who, before his death in January 1941, reasserted his solidarity with his persecuted brethren; and Proust, France's greatest twentieth-century novelist, also of Jewish extraction, who was anathematised by fanatical collaborationists as the chronicler of social decadence and homosexuality.

Von Ebrennac resolves the conflict between soldierly duty to acquiesce and the humanist values in which he believes by a quasi-suicidal request to be returned to active service, and prepares to leave for the Eastern front. Even the 'good' German cannot find it within himself to resist the Nazi machine. 'Ils se soumettent tous. Même cet homme-là' (**58**), concludes the uncle, drawing the political moral of the story. The ritualistic 'je vous souhaite une bonne nuit' is accompanied by an 'Adieu' to which the niece responds, breaking her silence for the first—and last—time (**59**).

*Le Silence de la mer* gives expression to a mode of resistance—silence—which recalls Jean Texcier's *Conseils à l'occupé* in the summer of 1940:

> Ils sont vainqueurs. Sois correct avec eux. Mais ne va pas, pour te faire bien voir, au-devant de leurs désirs. Pas de précipitation. Ils ne t'en sauraient au surplus aucun gré.

> Tu ne sais pas leur langue, ou tu l'as oubliée. Si un d'eux t'adresse la parole en allemand, fais un signe d'impuissance et, sans remords, poursuis ton chemin.[23]

These precepts are enacted almost to the letter in the uncle's reception of the German advance party—'ils me parlèrent, dans ce qu'ils supposaient être du français. Je ne comprenais pas un mot. Pourtant je leur montrai les chambres libres. Ils parurent contents' (**19**)—and acquire their ultimate expression in the couple's refusal to speak to von Ebrennac. Their silence, the niece's 'visage sévère' and inflexible disposition, are maintained, like French honour, to the end. Her 'Adieu' is a charitable recognition of his defeat: the only course open to him is to leave France. The story ends as it began, before the German(s). Life goes on.

And yet the text also contains the matrices of an alternative interpretation. The couple's positive refusal to acknowledge the German may appear negatively acquiescent; if they do not help him, nor do they hinder him. Indeed their 'accord tacite' appears to give effect to the Pascalian semi-proverb that 'tout le malheur des hommes vient d'une chose, qui est de ne savoir pas demeurer en repos, dans une chambre'.[24]  Moreover, to shun von Ebrennac is a serious step for the uncle: 'je ne saurais sans souffrir offenser un homme, fût-il mon ennemi' (**25**). Though their united front is maintained, he imparts his scruples to his niece—'c'est peut-être inhumain de lui refuser l'obole d'un seul mot' (**29**)—whose interrupted music suggests her own ambivalence towards things once loved, perhaps lovable again. 'Quelle nécessité intérieure', asks the uncle, hearing von Ebrennac play and thinking it is the girl, 'pouvait bien l'avoir soudain décidée?' (**35**). The price of her resistance is inner conflict, a 'drame intime soudain dévoilé' (**50**) whose physical manifestations are intense—'je vis, à la limite du front et de la chevelure, non pas naître mais jaillir, oui, jaillir, des perles de sueur' (**58-9**)—and which prompts his chastening admission that 'je me sentis soulevé par une absurde colère: la colère d'être absurde et d'avoir une nièce absurde' (**48**). Her 'Adieu', preceded by signs of lassitude, despair and by the 'offer' of her gaze (**52**), is not just a small, consolatory victory for von Ebrennac but recognition that his sojourn has been a privileged moment of their experience, to be regretted, not to be repeated, an 'occasion perdue'. Life may go on, but things can never be the same again: 'il me sembla qu'il faisait très froid' (**60**).

In retrospect, therefore, it is not difficult to see how commentators sensitive to textual ambiguities, and suspicious of the identity behind the pseudonym, produced a pro-collaborationist reading. One can also see why critical discussion dwelt so exclusively on von Ebrennac's credibility, a legitimate approach but one which underestimates the links between the character and his creator, and the considerable skills deployed by Vercors in creating a persuasive atmosphere of expectancy and involvement. Paradoxically, this approach has also diverted attention from the manner in which the text transcends its historicity, a more serious objection for the contemporary reader than criticisms based on the ideological verisimilitude of the protagonists. Until recent investigation by Margaret Atack and others, *Le Silence de la mer* arguably enjoyed the worst of both critical worlds: inadequate attention was given to its referential and representational qualities, its *mimesis,* and equally scant attention to its narrative and literary specificity, its *diegesis.* Clearly, however, a detailed understanding of the textual function demands that both be taken into account. For it seeks to subvert a prevailing orthodoxy (collaborationism) by defamiliarizing the reader: von Ebrennac may or may not be the German you expected, but in the last analysis they are all the same ('ils se soumettent tous'). Nevertheless it does so within familiar narrative and stylistic conventions which are not subversive but order-reinforcing, in contradistinction, for example, to Camus's *L'Étranger,* an ostensibly apolitical novel published 'legally' in 1942, whose 'impenitent' rejection of conventional literary codes establishes its ideologically transgressive nature.[25]

The extent to which *Le Silence de la mer* operates within a particular status quo may be seen in von Ebrennac's predilection for  essences, transcendence and myth. The idea that there exists 'une âme française', the special quality of the light in the fireplace, invested with spirituality by the objects on which it shines, the 'permanence' of a certain concept of the human condition, all these are semantic constructs which transform reality into verbal images and present as essential that which is accidental or contingent, as natural and permanent that which is historically determined and temporary. Writing of this distancing effect, S.B. John notes that: 'the "real" world is held in abeyance and what *lives* for us is a single stylized image: the firelight in the parlour, the almost palpable silence, and the stiff, embarrassed movements of uncle, niece, and von Ebrennac'.[26] The latter's criticisms of German absolutism (the fiancée dismembering the mosquito, its politicians whose values are little better, its 'inhuman' music), and his evocation of France as a necessary complement to Germanic coldness and emotional immaturity, are conveyed in a series of polarities—Chartres/ Nuremberg, spirit/ force, soul/absence of soul, Beauty/Beast—which universalise the situation, making it more accessible to the reader but more intellectually problematic. 'Le destin', he says, 'm'a conduit sur Chartres [...] dans une grande voiture blindée' (**39**), as if he had no personal responsibility for a war which he had previously linked to a promise to his dead father never to visit France 'avant d'y pouvoir entrer botté et casqué' (**28**). His inner conflict, though real, embodies the essentialist myth of *déchirement;* [27] if his final appearance in uniform marks his submission to the German military machine, his individual duty to decide where he stands once the mirage of collaborationism has been dispelled is metamorphosed into 'le Combat, —le Grand Bataille (*sic*) du Temporel contre le Spirituel' (**58**), and thereby denied. The sub-maritime imagery used to describe his conflict between love and duty, barbarism and civilisation, similarly metamorphoses individual choice and responsibility into a clash of elemental forces, of opposing and, by implication, historically equivalent systems: the Eastern front becomes 'l'enfer', the killing fields, 'ces plaines immenses' where, the narrator prophesies, 'le blé futur sera nourri de cadavres' (**58**).

Denial and mythicisation are also present in von Ebrennac's reminiscences about his fellow-student and room-mate at Stuttgart and Nuremberg:

> 'C'était mon frère. [...] Nous ne faisions rien l'un sans l'autre: je jouais devant lui ma musique; il me lisait ses poèmes. Il était sensible et romantique. Mais il me quitta. Il alla lire ses poèmes à Munich, devant de nouveaux compagnons. C'est lui qui m'écrivait sans cesse de venir les retrouver. C'est lui que j'ai vu à Paris avec ses amis. J'ai vu ce qu'ils ont fait de lui!' (**56**)

Being articulated here is the idea of the loss of part of the self, the 'good' self, suborned, betrayed ('j'ai vu ce qu'ils ont fait de lui') by the forces of darkness. If only he had not listened to these new friends! if only I had not listened to him, not gone to Paris! The myth of elective affinities, of kindred spirits, 'brothers' cruelly separated, expresses a split in von Ebrennac's own personality and the impossibility of the consummation of his love for the niece; in the same way, her unconscious dehumanisation as she struggles to deny her feelings and as her facial features assume 'la moue tragique des masques grecs' (**59**) places her emotional conflict on a more mythical plane. Similar in effect, too, is the quotation from *Othello*, 'Éteignons cette lumière, pour ensuite éteindre celle de la vie' (**45**), which introduces the tragic climax replicated in the title of Cyril Connolly's English translation of the *récit*, *Put out the Light* (1944), these words are echoed in the Goethean *'welch' ein Licht!'* with which von Ebrennac greets the niece's gaze (**52**), and the plangent 'Nevermore' from Poe's 'The Raven' with which he accepts the reality of Nazi plans to extinguish the 'light' of the French spirit (**55**). The originality of *Le Silence de la mer* was of course that in portraying that descent into darkness it was lighting a beacon of hope, but that paradox merely reinforces the ambiguities within it.

Few texts of comparative length and significance are so literary. Literature is a defining part of von Ebrennac's humanism and his European culture; it exists within his monologue as 'story' in its own right, a tale within a tale (he refers to Rostand's *Princesse lointaine* and to *Beauty and the Beast*); and literary references and allusions belong to the text's sign system and thematic structure:

> Il était devant les rayons de la bibliothèque. Ses doigts suivaient les
> reliures d'une caresse légère.
> — '...Balzac, Barrès, Baudelaire, Beaumarchais, Boileau, Buffon...
> Chateaubriand, Corneille, Descartes, Fénelon, Flaubert... La Fontaine,
> France, Gautier, Hugo... Quel appel!' dit-il avec un rire léger et hochant
> la tête. 'Et je n'en suis qu'à la lettre H!... Ni Molière, ni Rabelais, ni
> Racine, ni Pascal, ni Stendhal, ni Voltaire, ni tous les autres!...' (31)

Von Ebrennac's admiration for France's great writers provides him
with a convenient pretext for embarking on a survey of the
emblematic figures of other European civilisations, Dante,
Shakespeare and the inevitable Goethe, and thence to the spiritual
complementarity of France's literary and Germany's musical riches.
The litany of names, recalled in the triad of authors cited (Péguy,
Proust, Bergson) when the true nature of collaborationism is
revealed, also contributes to the incantatory quality of a 'monologue'
intended to charm the spirits of the hearth and overcome the silence
of his hosts. And the visual, almost visionary image of him standing
before the shelves is recaptured at the height of his inner conflict:

> Son regard passa par-dessus ma tête, volant et se cognant aux coins de
> la pièce comme un oiseau de nuit égaré. Enfin il sembla trouver refuge
> sur les rayons les plus sombres, — ceux où s'alignent Racine, Ronsard,
> Rousseau. (55)

By portraying von Ebrennac as a trapped bird, Vercors suggests a
noble being destroyed by the sordid reality of Nazism, the antithesis
of the civilisation represented by the masterworks of literature. But
the shadow of an ambiguity is also present on these 'rayons les plus
sombres'. Is some literature more, or less, than a refuge? Is its
capacity to disturb as important as its capacity to fulfil? This chapter
examines these and other questions, some of which can usefully be
approached through the genesis of the story as recounted by the
author.

## Genesis and composition

*La Bataille du silence* and *Les Occasions perdues* reveal the long-
standing and more immediate historical circumstances upon which
Vercors drew when he embarked on the composition of the *récit* in
1941. Among the former are Bruller's preoccupation with peace
between the wars, and his hope that France and Germany might be
reconciled in their common civilisation of artists and musicians (**BS**,
20-2), an attitude mirrored by a German 'ancien de Verdun' met on
a skiing holiday at Montana (*ibid.*, 23-4). A Briandist element is
present here, and more residually in the account of Bruller's trip to

Prague in 1938, in which images of 'old' Nuremberg sit uneasily beside the sinister new Reich (*ibid.*, 31-41). The same cities, and a hint of the same critical juxtaposition, occur in von Ebrennac's monologue: 'Pour un Allemand', he says, Nuremberg 'est la ville qui dilate son cœur parce qu'il retrouve là des fantômes chers à son cœur, le souvenir dans chaque pierre de ceux qui firent la noblesse de la vieille Allemagne' (**39**; my emphasis). In an indirect recall of the chauvinistic ('anti-Boche') attitudes of the young Bruller, he comments that 'j'étais un enfant à l'autre guerre et ce que je pensais alors ne compte pas' (**27**). His insect-hating fiancée recalls the German nursemaid who worked (briefly!) for the writer's family in the 1930s (**OP**, 83). More movingly recalled is the Jewish girl Stéphanie, for whom Bruller's intense adolescent passion expressed itself in silence and music, and in memory of whom he claimed to have embarked on the path of fiction: 'de quoi aurais-je écrit, si ce n'était de l'amour perdu?' (*ibid.*, 211). Since Stéphanie later died in Auschwitz (**BS**, 241-2), the element of nostalgia and loss present in what is already a retrospective account is doubly important. In several central respects *Le Silence de la mer* is the story of a lost love, an 'amour impossible'.

More circumstantial details were provided by the artist's return to his home at Villiers-sur-Morin in August 1940 and his encounter with its German occupiers. The Germans had treated the house carefully and were complimentary to its owners: 'cette maison a une âme' (**OP**, 206; **31**). Yet Vercors later found himself silently refusing to acknowledge their presence in the manner which was to characterise the uncle and the niece (**BS**, 146). There are resemblances of detail between the Germans' departure from Villiers and their arrival in the *récit:* 'un troufion vert-de-gris apparaît [...], une grande voiture blindée passe le porche' (**OP**, 206); 'D'abord deux troufions [...]. ... un torpédo militaire, gris et énorme, pénétra dans le jardin' (**19**). And a conversation overheard between two Germans in a café and reported to Vercors in terms reminiscent of Racine's *Britannicus* (IV. iii) revealed the true purposes of the *Kollaboration* — 'j'embrasse mon rival... pour l'étouffer... nous les bernons' (**OP**, 228-9) — and provided the essential *affabulation* for the story (*ibid.*).

Real-life models such as the Francophile Wehrmacht officer Ernst Jünger, author of the much-admired *Falaises de Marbre* and *Jardins et Routes*, and the German ambassador Otto Abetz, contributed to the portrayal of von Ebrennac (**OP**, 228). Others were found after the event. Of the literary censor in Paris, Lieutenant Gerhard Heller, who used his position to help Resistance suspects such as Jean Paulhan, Mauriac wrote: 'il a été merveilleux pour nous, ce type-là, vous savez, un peu l'officier du *Silence de la mer*'.[28] There are resemblances too, no doubt fortuitous, between von Ebrennac and Karl Heinz Bremer, *Lektor* at the École Normale Supérieure before the war, deputy director of the Institut d'Allemagne in 1941, killed on the Eastern front in May 1942. Manifestly, however, Vercors was giving expression to aspects or virtualities of his own personality and his own preoccupations. Von Ebrennac is an artist who shares Vercors's taste for Shakespeare and Poe, and although his medium is different, he too is an active creator, not a mere 'exécutant' (**28**). The presence of such traits does not nullify criticisms of von Ebrennac's verisimilitude, but in part explains it: the character is a 'double', separate, but insufficiently differentiated perhaps, from his creator.

The personal, projective element extends to detail which helps enlist the reader's sympathy. As we have recorded, Vercors injured a leg during the *drôle de guerre;* von Ebrennac inherits the 'jambe raide' (**23**) which the reader surmises to be the result of combat. His name, 'entièrement forgé' according to Vercors (**BS**, 342) despite the linguistic proximity of the French/German *brennen/brul(l)er*, invites the narrator to attenuate a potentially hostile reaction by suggesting a Huguenot strain (**22**). This recalls the author's religious antecedents, while the Gascon suffix *-ac* subliminally reinforces the unstated setting. For if the story has a location, it is the Charente where Vercors spent that week 'en famille' between his demobilisation and his return to Meaux in August 1940.

It is true that the text eschews precise geographical detail, and its French protagonists have no obvious local particularisms. But von Ebrennac, it will be recalled, mentions the reception given to his troops in Saintes (**32**), close to the limit of German advance in the south-west and the demarcation line between the occupied and unoccupied zones, while the 'longue maison basse, couverte de treilles, aux vieilles tuiles brunes' (**24**), though modelled on Vercors's home at Villiers (**BS**, 201; 210; 340), has a distinctly meridional flavour. Such details, together with references to the unseasonal November temperature (**21**) and the onset of the 'longs jours printaniers' which coincide with von Ebrennac's visit to Paris (**43**), create a valuable impression of time and place, though, as I shall argue, a sense of timelessness is also significant for the impact of the story.

## Characters and characterisation

In his *Wehrmacht* uniform and towering physical stature, von Ebrennac represents the intrusion of conquering reality on the domestic intimacy of the French couple and embodies the political choice they face: to collaborate or to resist. 'Immense et très mince, [...] le profil puissant, le nez proéminent et mince' (**22**), his traits almost caricature the Aryan superman:

> Ses hanches et ses épaules étroites étaient impressionnantes. Le visage était beau. Viril et marqué de deux grandes dépressions le long des joues. On ne voyait pas les yeux, que cachait l'ombre portée de l'arcade. Ils me parurent clairs. Les cheveux étaient blonds et souples, jetés en arrière, brillant soyeusement sous la lumiere du lustre. (*ibid.*)

Strikingly, however, some of the same details also create an air of pervasive and disquieting unreality. The initially unseen eyes, his slight stoop (he is described as 'voûté'), the facial 'dépressions' and the 'ombre portée par l'arcade' suggest a burden of melancholy out of keeping with his hopes for a Franco-German 'marriage' but consistent in terms of plot and theme with his subsequent disillusionment. Like other details to be examined later, this initial portrayal suggests that the ending of the *récit* is written into its beginning, notwithstanding the writer's claim that as late as September 1941 he was still 'hesitating' about the outcome, before rejecting the '"happy end" trop peu conforme à la mentalité allemande' in favour of 'l'adieu désespéré que l'officier obéissant adresse à ses hôtes, brisant un cœur prêt à l'aimer' (**OP**, 229).

When he appears in civilian clothes, the impression conveyed is also one of quality and substance:

> Le pantalon était d'épaisse flanelle grise, la veste de tweed bleu acier enchevêtré de mailles d'un brun chaud. Elle était large et ample, et tombait avec un négligé plein d'élégance. Sous la veste, un chandail de grosse laine écrue moulait le torse mince et musclé. (**26**)

Similar descriptions underline the sense of ease and relaxed self-possession which increasingly disconcerts his hosts: 'Il portait toujours son pantalon de flanelle grise, mais sur le buste une veste plus légère en jersey de laine couleur de bure couvrait une chemise de lin au col ouvert' (**42**). The change into civilian clothes distances von Ebrennac from German militarism; his musicianship and culture distance him from Nazi barbarism. His return to combat endorses the reality of both, and makes Vercors's point doubly effective.

Other details—his fine white teeth, the 'mains longues, fines, nerveuses' (**35**), little mannerisms such as stroking the occipital bone 'd'un mouvement naturel de cerf' (**28**), nodding as if to emphasize an idea which gives him pleasure (**32**)—create an individuality which his subsequent conflict will confirm and destroy; they also help to make him a likeable, potentially attractive 'suitor' for the niece. His voice is described as 'assez sourde, très peu timbrée. L'accent était léger, marqué seulement sur les consonnes dures. L'ensemble ressemblait à un bourdonnement plutôt chantant' (**27**).

Several successive references (**30-31**; **33**; **36**), to 'sa voix sourde aux infléxions chantantes' (**47-8**) suggest that the narrator is appreciative in spite of himself. Since only von Ebrennac speaks in seven months, it is natural that his voice should be the focus of such attention, but its attractiveness further underlines his presence and the sense of familiarity we develop with him.

It is tempting to see in Vercors's largely descriptive characterisation the imprint of his original artistic calling, a point developed by Konstantinović (**VED**, *passim,* esp. pp. 135-40). The author himself claimed that the decision 'de ne jamais faire comprendre un personnage par une description introspective' (**BS**, 185) reflected a literary influence: Conrad. Yet apart from the final passages which evoke von Ebrennac's inner turmoil, the metaphysical density of Conrad's creations and the *chiaroscuro* in which his characters exist are absent from the sober, more limpid lines of Vercors's *récit*. Considerable emphasis is indeed placed on exterior signs (gestures, hand movements, other facial and bodily indications), but the need to convey the French couple's reaction to von Ebrennac's 'interminable monologue' by non-verbal means was unquestionably more significant than an otherwise notional literary filiation.

The narrator is one of the protagonists and, within the conventions of the genre, unlikely to reveal his personality, his attitudes or background in a systematic way, far less offer us personal description. The young woman, likewise, is known to him: the relatively few physical details or character traits which emerge do so in accordance with the requirements of the developing story. It is through von Ebrennac's eyes that we first see her 'pur profil, têtu et fermé' (**3 3**), and her 'nuque frêle et pâle d'où les cheveux s'élevaient en torsades de sombre acajou' (**41**). It is when she looks at her uncle as if in reproach that we learn her eye colour: 'il me sembla lire dans ses beaux yeux gris un reproche et une assez pesante tristesse' (**48**). Only the outsider von Ebrennac enjoys full descriptive characterisation as well as the active, self-revelatory attribute of speech, an attribute which further invests him with the status of auxiliary narrator. He characterises the furnishings in the room—'on ne dit pas: voilà des merveilles' (**33**)—and details the impressive personal library; he informs us that the uncle is an old man (**32-3**), and it is by comparison with his own considerable height that the uncle's is revealed: 'moi je ne me cognerais pas même le sommet de la tête' (**27**). Vercors's surrender of the authorial third-person point of view, omniscient and apparently 'objective', in favour of a first-person, possibly subjective, narrator pays considerable dividends in textual realism and persuasiveness.

We quickly form the impression that we know the narrator well.

His pipe-smoking and reading suggest a professional, middle-class and not an agricultural or industrial background, an inference supported by the erudition of his comparisons: von Ebrennac reminds him of Louis Jouvet; hand movements recall 'certaines figures des danses religieuses de Java' (**57**); his niece's lips, 'pareilles aux bords d'un vase d'opaline [...], esquissaient la moue tragique des masques grecs' (**58-9**). He does not appear to work and is presumably retired, a reasonable supposition given his notional age, though judging by his modest life style his means are not substantial: his is not the 'château' originally destined for von Ebrennac and missed inadvertently by his aides (**24-5**). The revelation that they have 'peu de bois et encore moins de charbon' (**24**) evokes a historical situation recognizable to the majority of the population. His visit to the *Kommandantur* 'pour une quelconque déclaration de pneus' (**47**) suggests ownership of a car, but we never see it and he was clearly not an essential user (doctor, for example). This is the only time we see the Frenchman on von Ebrennac's 'territory', shortly after his return from Paris, and the episode is more important as a stage in the plot than for reasons of historical authenticity. Vercors himself records a visit to local German headquarters for travel documents (*Ausweis*) and petrol coupons before leaving Saintes (**BS**, 114). Perhaps, like his creator's old Ford which after the return to Paris 'rendit l'âme' (*ibid*.), the uncle's car has simply been consigned to the garage until better days...

The barn he uses as an *atelier* may indicate an amateur handyman or an artist, and another unstated parallel with Vercors, apprenticed to the joiner at Villiers in 1940-1941. The information that 'le café me fait dormir' (**21**), added by way of explanation of the evening routine, individualises him a little without suggesting a problematic eccentricity: the French protagonists must be as representative as possible, and the uncle, on whom we rely for our knowledge and understanding of events, must be trustworthy. The absence of an obvious political stance makes it easier for the reader to identify with him; nor is there any reference to possible war service in 1914-1918, which would have created very different intellectual and political parameters, as in 'L'Été à la Maurie', in which Chardonne's French householder and the German officer are 'anciens de Verdun'. The uncle's reflective tone, and the observant nature which we divine from the detail of his comments, suggest that he will be a credible witness. His mistake over the colour of von Ebrennac's eyes, subsequently corrected, helps to establish that credibility; the admission that 'j'appris ce jour-là qu'une main, pour qui sait l'observer, reflète les émotions aussi bien et mieux qu'un visage car elle échappe davantage au contrôle de la volonté' (**51**), gives final justification to the confidence the reader places in his interpretation of the other characters' inner conflicts.

He is also astute. By showing von Ebrennac's aides the rooms while pretending not to understand them, he avoids having to attempt a reply while sharing his quiet sense of superiority with the reader: the Germans do not realise that they cannot speak French ('dans ce qu'ils supposaient être du français'). His reflections on von Ebrennac's reasons for changing into civilian clothes allow the benefit of the doubt to the latter while preserving his own independence of judgement (**30**). His intuition is almost visionary: 'je sentais l'âme de ma nièce s'agiter' (**38**), 'il me semblait voir l'homme derrière la porte' (**49**). And from his first tentative judgement on von Ebrennac, 'Dieu merci, il a l'air convenable' (**23**) to the much more emphatic 'ma foi, je l'admirais' (**38**), he influences the reader's attitudes, fulfilling an important narratorial function we shall encounter in other stories.

Unnamed throughout, referred to habitually as 'ma nièce', the girl is a wholly silent participant, dependent on the narrrator to record her reactions and to divine her unvoiced feelings and moods. This he does with considerable sensitivity, despite an occasional generalisation—'les femmes ont une divination de félin' (**48**)— whose function is narratological rather than stereotypical. By opting for silence, she becomes an object in von Ebrennac's discourse rather than a partner in it. It is he who identifies the 'demoiselle silencieuse' (**32**) with France: 'Il faudra vaincre ce silence. Il faudra vaincre le silence de la France' (**33**); and it is he who characterises the relationship between France and Germany in the language of sexual love, united as in his dead father's wish like husband and wife (**28**), in 'un amour partagé' (**41**).

The sexual representation of Franco-German relations was scarcely new: the niece's literary antecedents include Barrès's *Colette Baudoche;* among her contemporaries is Hortense in 'L'Été à la Maurie'. But the identification of the respective countries/ protagonists with Beauty and the Beast, the latter metamorphosed into a handsome prince, gives it a particular prominence in *Le Silence de la mer*, as does language which, though not always circumlocutory—'maintenant j'ai besoin de la France' (**36**)—can be read on two levels. Von Ebrennac recognizes frankly that 'aujourd'hui et pour longtemps la France ne peut tomber volontairement dans nos bras ouverts sans perdre à ses yeux sa propre dignité' (**43**). Frank too is the assertion that, pending the establishment of a mutual partnership with Germany, someone prepared like Darlan to 'vendre sa patrie' was a necessary condition of their union: 'souvent la plus sordide entremetteuse est à la base de la plus heureuse alliance' (**43**). Unusually, there is no indication of the niece's reaction to such directness, which is related to von

Ebrennac's announcement of the trip to Paris and to his confident expectations for the future; his disillusionment means that the girl's feelings are never put to the test. This fact perhaps, as much as her strength of character, enables the story to be construed as a critique of collaborationist intellectuals such as Chardonne or Brasillach, who described Germany as their 'vieille maîtresse' and incurred particular odium at the Liberation for having 'slept' with the invader, a theme amplified by Sartre in his discussion of the submissiveness of some of his compatriots towards German domination.[29]

Sensitive however to the sexual sub-text, to the niece's 'anonymity' and to the 'menial' (domestic) tasks in which she is portrayed (serving the uncle's coffee, sewing), influenced also perhaps by the conventional quality of Vercors's other women characters (Madame Bufferand in *Ce Jour-là*, Madame Dacosta in *L'Imprimerie de Verdun*), students are sometimes inclined to see her as a passive, indeed subservient figure. This is not necessarily a false perception, given the other ambiguities in the story and von Ebrennac's status in the narrative, but it overlooks the fact that she initiates the resistance to him and shows fortitude in persisting in her stance despite the uncle's scruples. Moreover, that stance effectively dictates the activities she can conduct in von Ebrennac's presence; her silent sewing and knitting, like the uncle's reading, will prove increasingly difficult to concentrate upon and will acquire more symptomatic significance as the story unfolds. If there is a subordination, therefore, it arises arguably from the textual dynamics themselves, and from a complex positional interchange between the protagonists.

## Narratives of inclusion

By refusing to engage in conversation, the uncle and niece allow von Ebrennac to dictate the agenda; by reporting von Ebrennac's statements and speculating about his unvoiced feelings and motives, the narrator gives these greater relief. 'Était-ce pour nous épargner la vue de l'uniforme ennemi? Ou pour nous le faire oublier, — ou pour nous habituer à sa personne? Les deux, sans doute' (**30**). When von Ebrennac refers to *Macbeth*, 'je me demandais avec stupeur s'il pensait au même tyran que moi' (**43**). When he is delayed, the narrator notes that 'je m'agaçais de reconnaître qu'il occupait ma pensée' (**26**), while the non-resumption of his evening visits on his return from Paris prompts the admission that 'cette absence ne laissait pas mon esprit en repos. Je pensais à lui, je ne sais pas jusqu'à quel point je n'éprouvais pas du regret, de l'inquiétude' (**47**), feelings the more intense for being unacknowledged:

> Ni ma nièce ni moi nous n'en parlâmes. Mais lorsque parfois le soir
> nous entendions là-haut résonner sourdement les pas inégaux, je voyais
> bien, à l'application têtue qu'elle mettait soudain à son ouvrage, à
> quelques lignes légères qui marquaient son visage d'une expression à la
> fois butée et attentive, qu'elle non plus n'était pas exempte de pensées
> pareilles aux miennes. (**47**)

Pivotal in the development of the couple's sense of unease is the
motif of imprisonment, which first appears when, in a transparent
appeal for his listeners' sympathies, von Ebrennac likens himself to
the Beast, Beauty's 'geôlier' (**33**). There is ambivalence here: the
occupier is the jailer, but the point of the fable is of course that he
too is imprisoned in his condition, and needs her to liberate him. The
motif reappears in the image of von Ebrennac standing braced
against the lintel, his face seen through his outstretched arms,
'comme à travers les barreaux d'une grille' (**36**), and in his refusal
to succumb to the temptation to 'secouer cet implacable silence par
quelque violence de langage' (**38**). The semantically close meanings
of 'secouer le silence/secouer le joug' are confirmed by the sequel:

> Quand parfois il laissait ce silence envahir la pièce et la saturer jusqu'au
> fond des angles comme un gaz pesant et irrespirable, il semblait bien
> être celui de nous trois qui s'y trouvait le plus à l'aise. [...] Et moi je
> sentais l'âme de ma nièce s'agiter dans cette prison qu'elle avait elle-
> même construite, je le voyais à bien des signes dont le moindre était un
> léger tremblement des doigts. (**38**)

A crucial transition is taking place: von Ebrennac is not excluded by
their silence, they are imprisoned within it. The unintended,
paradoxical consequence of their adopted stance is their dependence
on the invader to liberate them...

Von Ebrennac's idealism, his ignorance of the realities of
Occupation, the lack of ironic distance or critical perspective which
might have been created by discussions with the old man and the girl,
ensure that the discovery of the true nature of collaboration is not
just a profound shock to him: it also shocks his French listeners and
further increases the reader's sympathetic identification with him.
This process has already been flagged by the narrator's 'je
l'admirais', but is also apparent in the changing terminology used to
refer to him. Predictably, the impersonal 'l'officier' occurs most
frequently in the early pages (ten times between pages 21 and 27, and
only three thereafter). The more dismissive 'l'Allemand' figures
only once (**23**), compared to the relatively neutral, unmilitary
'l'homme' (**27; 49**) and the full name (**38; 47**). On the one occasion
when the narrator actually addresses him, it is with the formal
imperative 'Entrez, Monsieur' (**50**), designed to acknowledge von
Ebrennac's presence at the door and to invite him to enter. But in the

dramatic and poignant final scene, distance and formality give way to
familiarity: the uncle reports that 'Werner respira' (**56**), 'les yeux de
Werner brillèrent' (**59**), suggesting an intimacy that the couple's
outward stance is to refuse, and his closeness to acceptance as the 'fils
d'un village pareil' which his conflict between duty and inclination,
not theirs, ultimately prevents.

The image of the niece conveyed in the first part of the *récit* is
one of silent inflexibility: 'ma nièce avait ouvert la porte et restait
silencieuse. Elle avait rabattu la porte sur le mur, elle se tenait elle-
même contre le mur, sans rien regarder' (**21**); 'le dernier mot [...]
tomba dans le silence. Ma nièce avait fermé la porte et restait adossée
au mur, regardant droit devant elle' (**22**); 'ma nièce ouvrit la porte
qui donne sur le petit escalier et commença de gravir les marches,
sans un regard pour l'officier, comme si elle eût été seule' (**23**).
Repetition reinforces the silence of indifference and suggests a
claustrophobia which is almost tangible to the reader as well as von
Ebrennac ('il sembla mesurer le silence'). Following the latter's
retiral for the night and the uncle's 'Dieu merci, il a l'air
convenable' (**23**), we read: 'Ma nièce haussa les épaules. Elle attira
sur ses genoux ma veste de velours et termina la pièce invisible
qu'elle avait commencé d'y coudre' (*ibid.*). Her sewing intimates her
desire to return to normality, and is an appropriate metaphor for the
silent understanding between them, and for the 'invisible' texture of
the story being unfolded.

For a month, the narrator records, von Ebrennac spends time
each evening on subjects whose common denominator was that 'ils ne
supposaient pas de réponse' (**25**). A cold snap marks a qualitative
change, the wintry conditions prompting him to seek the warmth of
the fire, and allowing him to evoke the rugged winters of his own
country and to say something more personal about himself. The girl
displays total absorption in her task: 'ma nièce tricotait lentement,
d'un air très appliqué' (**26**); 'ma nièce tricotait avec une vivacité
mécanique. Elle ne jeta pas les yeux sur lui, pas une fois' (**27**). When
von Ebrennac rhapsodises about France and Germany united 'comme
mari et femme', what meets his gaze is not a woman but a 'statue'
(**28**). And when, after his customary goodnight, the uncle avers
awkwardly that 'c'est peut-être inhumain de lui refuser l'obole d'un
seul mot', we read: 'ma nièce leva son visage. Elle haussait très haut
les sourcils, sur des yeux brillants et indignés. Je me sentis presque
un peu rougir' (**29**). Her attitude of resolve remains apparently
rigorous; in fact, a significant change is taking place, from shoulder-
shrugging indifference to eyebrow-raising indignation, from absence
of emotion to emotion.

The increasing tension between her will to resist and the
attraction she feels towards von Ebrennac is conveyed in a series of

variations on the motif of the sewing thread. When he expresses his
contentment at her silence, she blushes slightly, tugging 'un peu trop
vivement, trop sèchement sur l'aiguille, au risque de rompre le fil'
(**33**). Predictably, the latter eventuality occurs during von
Ebrennac's reminiscences about his fiancée and their walks in the
forest, though Vercors neatly avoids too direct a suggestion of
emotional cause and effect: 'il attendit, pour continuer, que ma nièce
eût enfilé de nouveau le fil, qu'elle venait de casser. Elle le faisait
avec une grande application, mais le chas était très petit et ce fut très
difficile' (**40**). Despite the narrator's charitable explanation of her
difficulties ('le chas était très petit'), this episode conveys her
increasing inability to concentrate. This is intensified after von
Ebrennac's return from Paris:

> Tout au long de la soirée elle ne cessa de lever les yeux de son ouvrage,
> à chaque minute, pour les porter sur moi; pour tenter de lire quelque
> chose sur un visage que je m'efforçais de tenir impassible, tirant sur ma
> pipe avec application. (**48**)

That she now looks to the uncle for some sign of encouragement or
explanation, while he seeks refuge in the studiously deliberate
activity ('avec application') which previously characterised her,
measures the transition which has taken place: 'A la fin, elle laissa
tomber ses mains, comme fatiguée, et pliant l'étoffe, me demanda la
permission de s'aller coucher de bonne heure' (**48**). The final scene
in which, her 'attention abolie', she distractedly attempts to wind
wool round her fingers as the ball unravels defiantly on the floor,
confirms her failure to maintain the unbroken fabric of their resolve
(**52**). There follows a gesture of impotent despair or surrender: 'la
jeune fille lentement laissa tomber ses mains au creux de sa jupe, où
elles demeurèrent penchées et inertes comme des barques échouées
sur le sable' (*ibid.*).

The image of the vessels reappears in a final expression of
tension, but it now draws von Ebrennac and the niece tautly together:
'Ses pupilles, celles de la jeune fille, amarrées comme, dans le
courant, la barque à l'anneau de la rive, semblaient l'être par un fil si
tendu, si raide, qu'on n'eût pas osé passé un doigt entrer leurs yeux'
(**59**). Separation and exclusiveness have given way to inclusiveness
and a curious binding (bonding). The fact that Cocteau's *La Belle et
la Bête* (1946) post-dated the *récit* invalidates inferences we might
draw about authorial intentionality, but for the post-war reader, the
niece's choice of a shawl decorated with a Cocteau-designed sequence
of hands '[qui] se désignaient mutuellement avec mollesse' (**49**) can
be read as symbolic of her assumption of the role she has struggled
to deny. It is true, as we shall see, that the identification which
occurs between them has a dramatic, apparently traumatic,
dimension. But it is in the same final scene that the habitual 'ma

nièce' is abandoned by the narrator for the apparently more detached but surely more compassionate term 'la jeune fille' (**52**; **5 9**), a change mirroring his use of the appellation 'Werner' and giving them an equality of status as his 'children'.

Triangularity is fundamental to the conflict between the couple's joint refusal to acknowledge von Ebrennac, and the growing feelings of respect (the uncle) and attraction (the niece) they individually harbour towards him. Arguably, therefore, their number and degree of kinship were determined by Vercors's didactic purposes. A father-mother-daughter or uncle-aunt-niece configuration would have sundered the narrative unity of the text, by creating two parental figures able to discuss events when the younger person was not present. By the same token, there would have been an alternative, conjugal form of private life with its own routines and another point of view on von Ebrennac. A mother-daughter or aunt-niece combination would have eliminated the stereotypical but important attributes of the masculine observer and created other complications, not least the need to explain the otherwise historically plausible absence of the male *chef de famille*. Dead? and if so, how? in the previous Franco-German conflict? a prisoner of war in the present one? A father-daughter combination, finally, might have created a further complication insofar as a father could have been less objective about the girl's changing feelings towards the German.

That the text invites such a reading is however suggested by the inadvertent assimilation of the uncle to a father-figure in students' work, a lapsus not unheard of among postgraduate scholars,[30] and by the atmosphere of intimacy created by the 'accord tacite' between uncle and niece, the warmth of the room in which they spend the winter, the evening routine of coffee, sewing, reading, and the special quality of the light which prompts von Ebrennac's 'cette maison a une âme'. Moreover the very idea of 'soul', like the 'silent sea' of the title, suggests absence/presence, and another form of triangularity: 'Mais qu'est-ce que l'auteur veut dire, avec son titre?' asked Vercors's printer. 'Pourquoi *Le Silence de la mer?* Moi je dirais plutôt le silence de la nièce. Pas vous?' (**BS**, 203). Apart from the homonyms *mer / mère* which justify Oudeville's quip as a play on words, and the Bachelardian resonances referred to by Frederick Harris,[31] the question pointedly underlines an absence in the lives of the three protagonists. In my view, the impact of *Le Silence de la mer* arises partly from the subliminal presence of this textual *non-dit*, whose effect is to 'write' von Ebrennac into the story by generating the missing common figure, the silent mother, 'la mer(e) silencieuse'.

Integral to this process is the fact that Vercors, though careful to mark the seasonal changes which occur during von Ebrennac's

seven-month stay (winter, spring, summer), makes no mention of
Christmas or Easter, important family occasions in non-practising
French households—here again the sparsity of sociological detail is
important—and, for believers, sacramental ones. The writer's
atheism, and the need not to give comfort to Vichy's climate of
Catholic revivalism more than adequately explain the absence of an
explicitly religious frame of reference, while the narrator's
speculation about von Ebrennac's Protestant antecedents offers no
clue to his own attitudes: *Le Silence de la mer* is not a theological,
far less a confessional work. Moreover, in purely practical terms,
the observation by uncle and niece of festivals of atonement and
reconciliation would have dictated a radically different handling of
the relationship with von Ebrennac. When the latter, at the height of
his inner conflict, 'regardait, avec une fixité lamentable l'ange de
bois sculpté au-dessus de la fenêtre, l'ange extatique et souriant,
lumineux de tranquillité céleste' (**58**), the serene indifference of
religion to the human drama being played out below seems
confirmed.

And yet the very presence of the angel, to which the reader's
attention is directed at the beginning as well as the end (**23**; **58**), von
Ebrennac's references to the soul and the inner presence of God
(**36**), the 'bourdonnement plutôt chantant' of his voice which, the
narrator observes, give his monologue 'la continuité monotone d'une
prière' (**31**), impart a tangibly spiritual quality to a story which
combines von Ebrennac's 'Bataille du Temporel contre le Spirituel'
with the contemplative atmosphere established by the French couple.
In this perspective, a detail mentioned in Vercors's account of his
return to Villiers in 1940, but omitted from the *récit,* is particularly
intriguing: a death-mask of Pascal, consigned to a cupboard by the
writer and found by the Germans, had been placed 'à l'honneur au
centre de la cheminée' (**BS**, 115). Had they mistaken Pascal for
Napoleon, as Vercors surmises? The fact that the episode is
mentioned again (*ibid.,* 146-7) and linked to the compliment paid to
Vercors and to von Ebrennac's hosts ('cette maison a une âme'),
suggests otherwise. Its omission from *Le Silence de la mer,* however
justified by the writer's need to keep his identity from family and
friends, reinforces the inference that part of the impact of the *récit*
arises from the existence of an unstated religious dimension, a textual
'repressed' in whose articulation the reader participates. The
plausibility of this hypothesis was corroborated by an inserted
flashback sequence in a BBC television adaptation, in which *three*
people, the uncle, the niece (wearing a crucifix necklace) and the
presumably since-deceased aunt, share a picnic of bread and wine.[32]
This reinstatement of the silent 'soul' of the house, the absent
mother-figure, is, I believe, one of the ways in which the text

simultaneously constructs a more complex representation of 'la Patrie' than that suggested by the equation between the niece and France, and transcends ideology.

## Poe and Shakespeare

As befits the climax of von Ebrennac's 'monologue', the ending of *Le Silence de la mer* is both highly literary and highly theatrical. The latter quality is emphasised by the 'trois coups pleins et lents, les coups assurés et calmes d'une décision sans retour' (**50**) with which he knocks at the door, and by the resemblances the narrator discerns with the actor Jouvet (**51**). But it is a function, too, of the apparent disproportion between what von Ebrennac has to reveal (the reality of collaboration) and the agonized manner of its revelation.

A mood of foreboding is established from the outset: 'Il pleuvait durement depuis le matin. Une pluie régulière et entêtée, qui noyait tout à l'entour et baignait l'intérieur de la maison dans une atmosphère froide et moite' (**49**). When the uneven tread descends the stairs, when the 'dernière marche eut crié' and a brief, pregnant silence falls, we divine the weight of von Ebrennac's 'exténuante épreuve' (*ibid.*). The uncle 'sees' him outside the door, heightening the tension and appealing to the reader's own imagination and senses (sight, hearing). Staring at the door-knob 'avec cette fixité inhumaine de grand-duc' (**50**), the niece presents a disquieting image of ducal aloofness and wide-eyed anticipation (unhyphenated, *grand duc* is a variety of eared owl), an image which would be almost predatory but for her evident signs of distress and vulnerability: 'elle était très pâle et je vis, glissant sur les dents dont apparut une fine ligne blanche, se lever la lèvre supérieure dans une contraction douloureuse'. The uncle's admission that 'devant ce drame intime soudain dévoilé et qui dépassait de si haut le tourment bénin de mes tergiversations, je perdis mes dernières forces' (**50**), underlines the harrowing nature of the experience for all three participants.

The scene begins with a confirmation of the narrative identification which has occurred between von Ebrennac and the niece. For if his entrance, 'plus que jamais en uniforme, [...] dans la ferme intention de nous en imposer la vue' (**51**), recalls his appearance at the start of the *récit,* his position and demeanour now replicate those of the girl on the evening of his arrival:

> Il avait rabattu la porte sur le mur et il se tenait droit dans l'embrasure [...]. Il resta ainsi quelques secondes droit, raide et silencieux, les pieds légèrement écartés et les bras tombant sans expression le long du corps, et le visage si froid, si parfaitement impassible, qu'il ne semblait pas que le moindre sentiment pût l'habiter. (**51**)

Portrayed thus in the open door, as if unable to enter or to withraw, having forced the couple to admit him but rooted to the spot as though he had intruded on their intimacy, von Ebrennac seems not so much devoid of human feelings as overpowered by their contradictory excess. His speech, when he breaks the silence, is uncharacteristically halting, as if the enormity of what he has to say is felt physically; his voice is 'plus sourde que jamais' (**52**), 'il respira, avec un effort d'asthmatique, garda un instant la poitrine gonflée... "il faut..." Il respira: "Il faut l'oublier"' (*ibid.*). Thereafter, however, the account of his disillusionment in Paris is delivered with a passionate, in places strident fluency: repetition, rhetorical questions, skilfully calculated breaks and pauses, verbal heightening that is typographically reinforced—'l'avez-vous MESURÉ?'; 'O Dieu! Montrez-moi où est MON devoir'(**56**; **58**)—and the '"oh" gémissant de l'amant trahi' (**57**) combine in what, in one less obviously distraught, might be considered a bravura performance.

His every silence and every gesture, from the exhausted but conventional 'puis il se prit les tempes et le front, écrasant ses paupières sous les petits doigts allongés' (**57**) to the more calculated arm outstretched 'vers l'Orient' announcing his departure 'pour l'enfer' (**58**), are captured by the narrator, whose descriptive powers are used to the full. The veins stand out on von Ebrennac's temples, his appearance is falcon-like (**51**) and yet he is being devoured. His 'front bourrelé et fripé', riven with anguish, resembles 'un grelin d'amarre' (**54**), his 'regard' frantically seeks an escape, 'volant et se cognant aux coins de la pièce comme un oiseau de nuit égaré' (**55**), he shakes his head 'comme un chien qui souffre d'une oreille' (*ibid.*), and his hands 'montèrent le long du corps, se livrèrent à la hauteur du visage à un incompréhensible manège qui ressemblait à certaines figures des danses religieuses de Java' (**57**).

The salvo of comparisons suggests that words are inadequate to express the nature and intensity of an experience which is traumatic as well as dramatic, yet the scene has both structure and direction, and the recurrent metaphors are not random. Von Ebrennac's inner tumult is exteriorized in a 'frémissement souterrain, comme fait un coup de brise sur un lac; comme, aux premières bulles, la pellicule de crème durcie à la surface d'un lait qu'on fait bouillir' (**54**). The volcanic contrast between surface and depth, the movement towards expression of powerful feelings partly denied, is prolonged in the evocation, 'sous la calme surface des eaux', of''la mêlée des bêtes dans la mer, [...] la vie sous-marine des sentiments cachés, des desirs et des pensées qui se nient et qui luttent' (**55**). These images of conflict also suggest petrification ('durcie') and immobilisation (stasis), traits reproduced in the 'yeux pâles et dilatés' (**54**) and stone-like countenance of the girl, as if she too were in the grip of the emotions of something seen: 'il ne bougea pas. Il restait tout à fait immobile, et dans son visage immobile et tendu, les yeux étaient plus encore immobiles et tendus, attachés aux yeux,—trop ouverts, trop pâles,—de ma nièce' (**59**). Only with her barely audible 'Adieu' does the tension finally drop, in a cathartic moment of release in which von Ebrennac's 'visage et tout son corps semblèrent s'assoupir comme après un bain reposant' (*ibid.*).

Von Ebrennac's implacable gaze into the girl's eyes expresses his imperative need for her to break a silence he has fought to overcome for seven months; only her farewell can break the spell she has cast upon him, only her words can permit him to depart, soothed if not fulfilled. Yet even allowing for the reality of his feelings and his over-idealistic view of Franco-German reconciliation, the intensity of the scene and the identification between them suggests an element of overdetermination, the displacement of emotions attendant on some other 'drame intime' whose presence the reader is made to feel, but not to understand. Vercors's use of literary allusion provides a clue. The end of the first phase of von Ebrennac's 'intolérable constatation' (**54**) is marked by the thrice-repeated 'Pas d'espoir!' and Poe's 'nevermore!':

> And the Raven, never flitting, still is sitting, still is sitting,
> On the pallid bust of Pallas just above my chamber door;
> And his eyes have all the seeming of a demon's that is dreaming,
> And the lamp-light o'er him streaming throws his shadow on the floor;
> And my soul from out that shadow that lies floating on the floor
> Shall be lifted—nevermore.[33]

As Konstantinović shows (**VED**, 26-7), Poe was one of Vercors's active preoccupations during the gestation of *Le Silence de la mer;* a volume of artwork completed in April 1942 included 'Silence', 'Ombre' and 'L'Île de la fée'. 'The Raven', familiar to the artist since his illustrations for the French version in 1930, tells of the loss of the loved one, Lenore, and the artist's crushing sense of grief and despair, evoked by the shadow/soul on the floor. Manifestly, von Ebrennac's emotions are those of irreparable loss (of his ideals and the possibility of the niece's love), the 'pallid bust of Pallas' above the poet's chamber door is paralleled in 'l'ange extatique et souriant' above the window in the *récit*, its deathly pallor that of the protagonist and the niece herself, 'd'une pâleur lunaire'.

Since Marie Bonaparte's psychoanalytic study of Poe (1933), it has been a critical commonplace to suggest that the poet's pallid women derive in part from the childhood memory of his dying mother. No such event marked Vercors's formative years, and his father, not his mother, died in 1930, the year in which he illustrated 'The Raven'; the importance of such data is narratological, not pathological. The elegy to the lost Lenore thematically and associatively reinforces the subliminal image of the 'mère silencieuse', the 'soul' of the house common both to the niece and to von Ebrennac, and gives the climax an important element of its affective power.

There is however a further sub-text whose presence shapes the scene and determines the reader's response to it, a text whose influence is more important for being unacknowledged and whose message is more commensurate with its theatricality. In re-enacting the 'betrayal' of which he was both witness and victim, von Ebrennac is phantasmatically reliving another event whose nature is suggested in one of the references to his staring eyes—'ses yeux s'ouvrirent très grands—comme sur un spectacle de quelque abominable meurtre' (57)—and whose original is identified in another story, L'Impuissance, 'a tale [...], whose lightest word / Would harrow up thy soul; freeze thy young blood; / Make thy two eyes, like stars, start from their sphere [sic]' (93). The secret sub-text of Le Silence de la mer is not Poe but Shakespeare, not Lenore but Elsinore, not Macbeth or Othello but Hamlet, which had fascinated Bruller since the 1920s and for which, after the defeat of 1940, 'j'entrepris, en même temps que j'écrivais Le Silence de la mer et fondais les Éditions de Minuit, cette illustration [...] que je n'avais jamais cessé de porter en moi' (H, viii).[34]

Bruller's illustrations for the play, begun in 1941-1942 and partly destroyed in a fire in 1953, remained unpublished until 1965, a life's work whose importance is underlined in the metaphor of gestation ('que je n'avais jamais cessé de porter en moi') used by the artist. But, unconsciously perhaps, he had already given literary expression to central themes of the play and to the 'amère délectation' (H, vii) which it inspired in him, in the work whose publication marked the 'birth' of the writer, Le Silence de la mer. The silence which envelops von Ebrennac like a 'brouillard' recreates the play's opening sense of nocturnal menace and melancholy; the ghostly apparition on the battlements, 'armé de pied en cap, sa visière levée' (H, 13), 'sous une lune blafarde' (ibid., 20), is recalled in the uniformed 'fantôme' whose arrival creates the story and whose 'Adieu' closes it. As in the play, the protagonist is a noble ('von') being of wide learning and culture, cerebral and sentimental, superior to and isolated from those around him, an unlikely warrior thrust by circumstance into an irreconcilable conflict between duty and inclination. Like Hamlet, von Ebrennac has made a promise to his dead father, only part of which (France's defeat in battle) he has been able to keep; the more important part (hope of national reconciliation), will be dashed by the visit to Paris, a betrayal which also occurs off-stage. Like the additional lines scripted by Hamlet for the 'play within the play', the theatrical climax of the *récit* invests von Ebrennac's betrayal with the emotions attendant on the original crime, writes it invisibly into the text and makes his dramatic soliloquy about the lights being extinguished an unwitting parody. *Le Silence de la mer*, finally, is also a tale of impossible love, the ghostly 'Adieu' also that of the niece, whose pallid vulnerability and disbelief echo the ill-fated Ophelia. And like the play, in which a queen's passion for her husband's brother, the hero's uncle, is almost more grievous than a king's murder, the mother is denied and yet reinstated. The complex triangularity whereby Claudius is a paternal surrogate for Hamlet, while Ophelia is more like a sister than a lover, is mirrored in the evolving relationships of the *récit* itself.

Von Ebrennac is a composite of Hamlet and the ghost (father and son). He is also a projection of his creator, Vercors alias Jean Bruller, failing to measure up to events in 1940: 'hésitant si le spectre qu'il avait vu était bien son père ou le diable, et ne pouvant se décider à tuer le roi assassin que dans le cliquetis aussi d'épées démouchetées, d'armes empoisonnées échangées dans la fureur, après que son indécision eut causé la mort inutile de Polonius et d'Ophélia, de Guildenstern, Rosencrantz, Laerte, la reine et lui-même' (**BS**, 62-3). *La Marche à l'étoile*, another story with tragic dimensions and explicit Shakespearian resonances (**145**), fictionalizes Vercors's father's life, prolonging it until the Occupation. It tells of Thomas Muritz's bitter realization that France and naturalised Frenchmen have been betrayed by their own compatriots. Vercors's conflict between pacifism and anti-fascism, and his ambivalence about the 'bataille postiche' of June 1940, have been recorded. Did a residual sense of guilt towards a dead father whose love for his adopted country might in retrospect have seemed greater than his own explain Vercors's identification with the pale Prince of Denmark, whose tragedy is frequently interpreted in Oedipal terms? If the sentiments expressed in *La Bataille du silence* are a true reflection of the author's sense of inadequacy in June 1940, it is possible to see how giving expression to the Hamlet myth in *Le Silence de la mer*, symbolically acting out the original betrayal, may be considered at one and the same time an act of resistance and a means of personal redemption. And if, as we have argued, the reinstatement of absent parental figures is part of the *récit*'s unconscious 'project', the subliminal Shakespearian dimensions of *Le Silence de la mer* are doubly significant. That the image of the 'silent mother' was an indissociable part of the writer's perception of the wartime writing and of his continuing preoccupation with *Hamlet* is confirmed by the scene in which he disclosed Vercors's identity to his family:

A ma femme, à ma mère, je ne fais que leur donner à lire, sans explication, à l'une *Le Silence de la mer* où notre maison se reconnaît, à l'autre *La Marche à l'étoile* avec le portrait de mon père. Je crois qu'une surprise un rien offensé paralyse un peu la première, malgré le secret si longtemps accepté. Mais tandis que, penché sur ma table à dessin, je travaille à mes estampes pour *Hamlet,* j'entends des pas discrets s'approcher sans bruit, et je reçois sur une tempe le baiser à peine appuyé, mais tendre et tremblant, de ma mère trop émue pour parler. Et puis elle se retire avec la même douceur et j'enferme dans mon cœur cette récompense muette. (**BS**, 340)

## The film and stage adaptations

Jean-Pierre Melville's film of *Le Silence de la mer* appeared in 1948, not without controversy.[35] It was shot in black and white on location at Villiers, with Jean-Marie Robain (the narrator), Nicole Stéphane and Howard Vernon in the principal rôles. The opening credit sequence shows a Paris street; a suitcase changes hands, from whose clandestine contents (the Resistance newspapers *Libération* and *Combat*), emerges a copy of the *récit*. The camera records the title page and dedication (the film ends, similarly, with the last lines, the date, October 1941, and the defiant *achevé d'imprimer,* so replicating the symmetry of the original). The narrative is prefaced by a flashforward in which the uncle-narrator recalls the events of the previous winter and the moral of the tale: 'ainsi, il était parti, ainsi il se soumettait lui aussi, comme tous les autres'. This device contributes to the carefully-paced treatment of the 'grand déploiement d'appareil militaire' (**19**), the successive advance parties preceding von Ebrennac's arrival: two harmless-looking soldiers in forage caps and greatcoats, the three horsemen who use the barn for temporary quarters, followed by the 'grand torpédo militaire' bearing kit and army trunk, and finally his orderly requesting sheets.

Set against a winter landscape, spare in its interior décor, faithful to the dialogue of the original, the film is enhanced by Edgar Bischoff's sombre if somewhat reedy musical score. A clock ticks sonorously, emphasising the silence. Among numerous visually neat touches which establish the mood, the uncle stretches out his fingers to the fire after noticing von Ebrennac's 'jambe raide' as the latter mounts the stairs, simultaneously conveying the evening chill, his own stiffness and vulnerability, and a suggestion of sympathetic identification with the German. In a scene whose stasis and understatement epitomize what Melville called the 'côté anti-cinématographique du récit' (*op. cit.*, p. 39), uncle and niece are profiled at the table, with steaming casseroles in the foreground, and von Ebrennac framed against the open garden door at the rear. Another sequence captures him outside the house, in the snow, listening to the couple's quiet laughter and conversation, the sounds of normal human sociability which his entrance invariably brings to an end. More innovative are the materialization of his entry into Chartres 'dans une grande voiture blindée' (**39**), as a Panzer commander lining up the tank's gun against, though not at, the distant profile of the cathedral, and a brief shot of the officer in tennis kit as the 'longs jours printaniers arrivent'. The sculpted angel is strikingly photogenic, and the niece's Cocteau-motif shawl adds emphasis to her 'Adieu'; effective too is the use of a quotation from Anatole France on the legitimacy of disobedience to criminal orders, left by the narrator for von Ebrennac before he departs, a feature also of the stage version.

Relatively modest departures from the temporal unities are taken considerably further in the spatial dimension. Melville creates a silent roadside encounter for the niece and von Ebrennac, and a final scene in which the latter is surprised by a knock on the door of his room which, he briefly surmises, might be one of his hosts (the girl?), only to be met with the smiling face and salute of his orderly. The most radical innovation is the developed treatment of the visit to Paris. We see von Ebrennac first of all 'en touriste', travelling in an open carriage round France's historic monuments (the Arc de Triomphe, the Carrousel, the Louvre, Notre-Dame), scenes intercut with wartime newsreel footage of the Places de l'Opéra, de la Concorde, etc. There is a wholly fictitious episode in a German officers' club, where he is apprised of the true nature of collaboration and where Teutonic ruthlessness is counterpointed sentimentally by an officer singing, minstrel-like, from a gallery. Other effects are less baroque. A newspaper clip of the Hitler-Pétain handshake at Montoire in October 1940, and a *Bekanntmachung* poster announcing the execution of twelve Communist and other hostages in reprisal for the 'lâche assassinat' of a German soldier, use appropriate historical detail and imaginative reconstruction to convey the ideological oppositions of the text. These are also expressed in von Ebrennac's silent reception in the café on his return from Paris, and developed more obliquely when the uncle pays a visit to the *Kommandantur* housed in the former *mairie,* whose Republican Marianne, displaced from her usual prominence, disconsolately faces a wall postered with collaborationist propaganda.

There are some losses, however, including the narrator's speculation about von Ebrennac's Huguenot origins, which might have been retained, and, more predictably, the figurative language and complex metaphorical associations of the climax. In von Ebrennac's announcement of his departure for the East, the prophetic and, by 1949, historically-consummated reference to 'ces plaines immenses où le blé futur sera nourri de cadavres' (**58**)

becomes simply the 'horizon'. Gone from his reading from *Macbeth*
to highlight Vichy's dilemma is the unvoiced irony of the narrator's
'je me demandais avec stupeur s'il pensait au même tyran que moi'
(**43**). Gone too is the reference to Darlan, 'votre amiral', replaced
by the more ambiguous term 'Président', an understandable change
for post-war audiences given Darlan's assassination in 1942 and
Laval's exclusive incumbency of the premiership ('Vice-Président du
Conseil') from April 1942 until 1944. Historical interval cuts both
ways: a reference to Treblinka, and the assertion by a fellow-officer
that by March 1941 the camp's targets had been met, is a grim
though not entirely successful means of evoking von Ebrennac's
ignorance of Nazi 'Nacht und Nebel'. The editing of the Paris
episode into two sequences flanking his final monologue is a
plausible structural feature, but it interrupts the peroration and
creates a conflation between spring and September (the date on the
poster seen on his return) which perhaps underlines Melville's
erroneous belief that von Ebrennac enjoyed two periods of leave in
the capital (*op. cit.*, p. 41). Nonetheless, the film is a generally
evocative encapsulation of the *récit*, parts of which have worn well.

Le Silence de la mer* was first staged in February 1949 at the
Théâtre Édouard VII in a production by Jean Mercure, and most
recently, by Jean Périmony at the Théâtre du Tourtour. The
directions specify *une pièce de séjour dans une maison à la
campagne, en juillet 1940*.[36] This is a more plausible date than the
hiatus between invasion and Occupation implied by the November
start of the *récit*, but it dilutes the power of the original, in which
von Ebrennac seemed to appear ghost-like out of the night, without
the compensatory wintriness of the film. Rather, a *porte vitrée,
translucide* (p. 175) provides a framework for *la silhouette de
l'officier, en cape et casquette* (p. 177). His 'immensity' is attenuated
in favour of a more neutral description: *l'officier, très grand,
claque des talons sur le seuil, salue militairement et se découvre*
(*ibid.;* my emphasis). Nor, inevitably, is there the same delay
between the advance guard's preparations and his arrival,
foreshadowed by a soldier bringing a trunk, by the off-stage sound
of armoured vehicles passing and *une chanson de marche allemande*
(p. 175), and by the niece's intimation to her uncle: 'Voilà. C'est fait.
Ils viennent d'amener les chevaux dans la grange. Un autre m'a
demandé des draps, il est déjà en train de préparer le lit' (p. 176).
Prior to this point, the uncle has been busy *à quelque travail qu'on
ne distingue pas bien* (p. 175); to no obvious gain, an *infusion*
replaces his evening coffee, sensibly reinstated in the 1990
production.
    Unlike the film, where voice-overs can be used to effect, the stage

adaptation requires a more obviously structured dialogue and verbal/non-verbal interaction between the French couple. In the *récit*, the uncle's 'c'est peut-être inhumain de lui refuser l'obole d'un seul mot' **(29)** prompted a visual response from the girl and a silent admission of regret by the narrator: 'Ma nièce leva son visage. Elle haussait très haut les sourcils, sur des yeux brillants et indignés. Je me sentis presque un peu rougir' (*ibid.*). The film retains the former and dispenses with the latter. The corresponding episode in the play blends direct speech, movement and physical contact:

> *La nièce le regarde, offusquée. Et lui, avec un sourire de repentir:*
> —Je n'ai jamais pu offenser un homme sans souffrir. Tu le sais bien.
> *Elle se lève, passe derrière son oncle, lui pose énergiquement les mains sur les épaules, le secoue gentiment—et il acquiesce par deux ou trois 'oui' de la tête. Elle l'embrasse avec tendresse. Pendant qu'elle va reprendre son ouvrage, la lumière baisse lentement jusqu'au noir.* (p. 182)

The girl's energetic but affectionate gesture makes her seem less passive, and adds a more obvious familiarity than is recorded in the original; this is one of a number of scenes which are effective theatre and appropriate adaptation. More questionable is the handling of the return from Paris. In both *récit* and film, the reader is prepared by von Ebrennac's failure to reappear downstairs, and by the scene at the *Kommandantur*. In the play, the German returns on a moonlit evening, 'en civil' but with his military cape over his arm and a travel bag: return, but perhaps also re-departure, are suggested. He lingers over the familiar objects in the room and, as if regretfully, handles the books:

> *A ce moment-là, par la porte du fond, entre l'oncle portant à la main une carabine. Il allume l'électricité, l'officier se retourne, l'oncle cache précipitamment l'arme derrière son dos. Ils se regardent longuement.* (p. 191)

Portrayed thus, von Ebrennac is merely a nocturnal intruder until identified, a potential threat to the household (the firearm is hurriedly hidden when the uncle recognizes him). Clumsy pathos is in danger of descending into burlesque when, in the immediate sequel following von Ebrennac's silent withdrawal, *l'oncle, un peu pétrifié*, [sic] *regarde longuement cette porte refermée, derrière laquelle la lumière s'est éteinte. Il va dissimuler son arme (soit derrière un rideau, soit de toute autre manière)* [sic]. This is weak stagecraft, suggestive merely of an old man's alarm and confusion, not the conflicting emotions shortly to be experienced in more extreme form by the girl:

> *Sa nièce entre à son tour. Elle aperçoit le sac de voyage et sursaute.*
> *Sans rien dire, le jeu de physionomie d'oncle et nièce révèle la question*
> *pathétique et muette de la jeune fille: Il est revenu? —et la réponse, non*
> *moins muette, embarrassée, compatissante, de l'oncle.* (p. 191)

Though quickly 'normalised' by von Ebrennac's limping gait
overhead (*au plafond, on entend les pas claudicants de Werner, le*
*va-et-vient d'un homme qui ne tient pas en place*), this silent *jeu de*
*scène* is at best an approximate answer to the problem of evoking the
niece's reaction to von Ebrennac's return, since her *sursaut*, like the
uncle's 'petrification', invites more than one interpretation.
Moreover, the unresolved question of the temporarily hidden
weapon returns after von Ebrennac's last exit, and this, as much
perhaps as the circumstances of the post-Liberation period,
determines the radically different closure of the play: with a smile of
encouragement to the niece, who responds with *un sourire aussi, qui*
*s'éclaire, s'accentue, rayonne'* (p. 198), the uncle deliberately
(*ostensiblement*) places the rifle on the table as the curtain falls. The
1990 production added the sound of the 'Chant des partisans', as von
Ebrennac's departing footsteps were replaced by the increasing tread
of 'l'armée de l'ombre'.

In its own terms, Jean Périmony's interpretation was professional
and imaginative, the intimacy of the small, vaulted, undergound
auditorium was eminently suited to most of the action, and the cast
were applauded to the echo (Périmony himself played the uncle, with
Métilde Weyergans and Philippe Palanque). Excellent use was made
of décor and spatial positioning, the niece separating the uncle and
von Ebrennac in the early scenes, and the uncle occupying the central
position in the later ones. But the most sensitive performances and
the inherent theatricality of the climax cannot entirely compensate
for the inadequacies of physical visuality compared with the *recit's*
powers of imaginary heightening, or wholly resolve the problems
presented by the transliteration to a different medium of a work
which has silence as its core, and other stories as its unvoiced sub-
text. In a judgement of the 1949 production which is a measure of
these difficulties and of the skill the writer displayed in the original,
Vercors wrote as follows:

> Manque-t-il donc quelque chose? Eh oui: il manque *ce que je n'ai pas*
> *écrit.* Ce qui, dans la nouvelle, suinte du silence comme à travers un
> filtre, ce qui s'y trouve celé de sentiments violents. A la lecture, les
> discours de Werner s'entendent par les yeux, ne troublent pas ce qui
> s'agite sous cette pesanteur muette. Au théâtre, ces mêmes discours
> emplissent la scène et la salle. Le silence, personnage principal, n'y fait
> que des trous, des intervalles. Tout ce qui reste, ce sont trois comédiens
> ensemble, pleins de talent, et des paroles. (**NJ**, 159; author's emphasis)

# Chapter Three

# Other Stories

Vercors's wartime stories contain a variety of situations, embedded to a greater or lesser degree in a recognizable historical reality, and a variety of characters, from the child in *Ce Jour-là* to the older narrator in *Le Silence de la mer*, from the garrulous printer in *L'Imprimerie de Verdun* to the idealistic and strangely superstitious Czech in *La Marche à l'étoile.* There is also diversity of exterior and interior décor: wooded, mountainous countryside forms the backdrop to the father and son's walk in *Ce Jour-là;* a sunbaked village is the location of *Désespoir est mort;* the booklined walls and the harmonium in *Le Silence de la mer* contrast with the more typically artisanal surroundings of Dacosta's little flat in the fifteenth arrondissement of Paris in *L'Imprimerie de Verdun,* and the nightmarish landscape of the camps in *Le Songe.* Characters also display a degree of differentiation in speech commensurate with the requirements of realism and their *raison sociale.* Vendresse's pithy colloquialisms and occasional intemperance of thought and language—'ce gros porc de Paars est un infâme salaud. J'ai été con' (**125**)—contrast with the more fluent disquisitions of Renaud, a connoisseur of literature and the arts despite his volatile temperament, in *L'Impuissance,* and the measured, often erudite reflections of the uncle in *Le Silence de la mer.* Predictably, however, closer inspection reveals deeper ideological, thematic and stylistic continuities beneath the surface dissimilarities. Like the different pieces in Claude Aveline's *Le Temps mort,* or Camus's post-war anthology, *L'Exil et le Royaume,* undertaken partly as 'exercices de style' to extend the writer's range, all of Vercors's stories are unmistakably from the same pen. He himself recalled how *La Marche à l'étoile,* written under a different pseudonym 'pour faire nombre' (**NJ**, 31) and in what purported to be a different style from *Le Silence de la mer,* was submitted to Paul Éluard on behalf of a fictitious third party, and promptly recognized for what it was, 'un récit de Vercors'(*ibid.*).

The most important of these recurrent features derives from the didactic intentionality of stories devised as exercises in persuasion if not in propaganda. Collectively they are an expression of resistance as well as individual accounts of resistance, but resistance is not their starting point. In each case, their protagonists undergo what Margaret Atack usefully describes as a 'transition from ignorance to knowledge', [37] apprehending the need for a particular reponse to circumstances and for a reassessment of beliefs and values. In *Désespoir est mort,* the narrator and two companions are brought together by the humiliation of defeat to find hope and, by implication, the will to continue the fight. Von Ebrennac's return to active service invites the conclusion that even well-intentioned Germans will ultimately bow to the system. Vendresse comes to see the realities of Pétainism by the fate of his Jewish employee, and following his initial endorsement of the régime, joins the Resistance (*L'Imprimerie de Verdun*). With the exception of *Désespoir est mort*, this process is usually triggered by an event which is external to the narrative locus, an 'off-stage' occurrence: it is in Paris that von Ebrennac's disillusionment takes place, Bernard Meyer suffers martyrdom in Silesia, and Vendresse arrives just too late to prevent the arrest of Madame Dacosta and her children. Dependent on outside stimulus, such characters are not initiators or innovators; moreover, their own naïveté is often partly responsible for the tragedies which befall themselves and others. Von Ebrennac's idealistic ignorance of the realities of Nazism—'Nous ne sommes pas des musiciens!' he is told (**53**)—is echoed in Vendresse, whose willingness to trust Pétain in defiance of the evidence leads him to dismiss Dacosta's well-founded fears, with lamentable consequences. Thomas Muritz only realizes the extent of his wilful self-delusion— 'un mot contre la France et vous savez ce qu'il devenait' (**188**)—when confronted with the fact that the men rounding up himself and his fellow Jews are French gendarmes, not German troops.

Invariably, therefore, the stories display a two-part structure, corresponding to the before/after division characteristic of *Le Silence de la mer*, which in one other important respect, the presence of a first-person narrator involved in but able to distance himself from the action, may be considered a template for the later works. The narrator in *Désespoir est mort* speaks from a fictional present post-dating the events the story purports to relate; like the narrator of *L'Impuissance*, he is a survivor who has lived to fight another day. In *L'Imprimerie de Verdun*, in which the chief protagonists perish, this function is doubly important since the narrator is also a Resistance agent whom Vendresse contacts with a view to engaging in the clandestine activity which costs him his life. Other narratorial functions include the traditional ones of providing information about the characters, often about their past lives, and bringing news of events to the reader. Here, though, omniscience may falter with regard to some detail or other, as in *L'Impuissance*—'si j'avais su... mais je ne savais pas' (**91**)—or in *L'Imprimerie de Verdun*, where narratorial ignorance is used to move the action forward: 'Comment s'était-il douté qu'il trouverait secours auprès de moi? Je n'en sais rien. Peut-être parce que naguère je prenais toujours le parti de Dacosta contre lui. En tout cas, c'est chez moi qu'il sonna ce matin-là. Ses yeux!' (**128-9**). The last two words remind us that the narrator also influences our perception of personalities and events, usually in the form of descriptive characterisation, as when Vendresse is seen in the throes of anguish about the fate of the family he had promised to protect: 'Je voyais son dos. Un brave large dos bonasse et un peu voûté. Je ne voyais pas ses mains, mais au mouvement des bras on devinait qu'il les serrait et desserrait' (**132**). An appeal may be direct:

> Est-ce que cela ne vous a jamais tourmenté? Quand, dans les jours heureux, allongé au soleil sur le sable chaud, ou bien devant un chapon qu'arrosait un solide bourgogne ou encore dans l'animation d'une de ces palabres stimulantes et libres autour d'un 'noir' fleurant le bon café, il vous arrivait de penser que ces simples joies n'étaient pas choses si naturelles. (**73**)

The function of this opening paragraph is to prepare the reader for the revelation of the unnatural in its most grisly contemporary form, the Nazi extermination camps whose reality the narrator of the tale has been reluctant to accept. But Vercors's intention is also to establish a sympathetic understanding, if not indeed a guilty complicity, with the reader, the narrator's alter ego, his extratextual 'double', a relationship replicated within the stories themselves. In *Le Songe,* the narrator says of his new companion that 'je ne parlais pas à un inconnu. [...] Nous nous connaissions très bien et toutes sortes de souvenirs communs nous liaient' (**76**), before the familiar but unknown figure metamorphoses into Yorick, identifying the narrator as Hamlet and leaving him with a smile, 'un signe fraternel' (**84**). The same story confirms the disturbing duality, recognising that 'l'homme n'est pas seul dans sa peau, il y loge une bête qui veut vivre' (**85**).

*La Marche à l'étoile* contains a number of narratorial interventions, from the initial series of interrogations: 'Qui fut coupable envers Thomas? Poignarda son amour et sa vie? L'envoya affronter la mort avec son âme en ruine? Faut-il accuser la France?' (**145**) to the concluding, damning, and unanswerable question addressed to the deity:

> Mon Dieu, pourquoi n'avez-vous pas aveuglé Thomas jusqu'à la fin? Pourquoi voulûtes-vous qu'en la brève seconde de ce dernier regard il aperçût ce visage horrible,—ce visage que nous portons en nous tous—nations ou hommes,—celui de la part désespérée qui fut toujours à Mammon? (**190**)

As this example suggests, some of these stories offer quite explicit generalisations about human actions, the nature of man and his relationship with the universe which foreshadow Vercors's more philosophical post-war writing. That this writing was determined by Vercors's continuing reflections on the horror of the Nazi experience is beyond doubt, but not our chief preoccupation here. This final chapter is devoted to three of the wartime pieces, *Désespoir est mort,* *L'Imprimerie de Verdun,* and *L'Impuissance.*

## Désespoir est mort

*Désespoir est mort* was written towards the end of 1942, some two
and a half years after the events it describes—'il y a trente mois, je
désirais la mort' (**7**)—and first appeared in 1943 in *Chroniques
interdites* under the pseudonym 'Santerre' (changed to the now
familiar 'Vercors' when the volume was reissued in 1945). Like other
stories in the collection it reflects the author's wartime experiences;
unlike *Le Silence de la mer,* it deals not with the problems of
occupation but with France's military humiliation in 1940, and
notably with the 'bataille postiche' in which Vercors participated
during the strange hiatus between the signature of the armistice and
the cessation of hostilities. It was, the narrator records, a 'déshonorant
simulacre qui nous en avait plus appris, en ces trois jours serrés entre
deux armistices, sur l'infamie dérisoire de certains hommes couverts
d'honneur, que l'expérience de toute une vie' (**9**). The story tells of
how the narrator overcame these feelings and found new hope.

   This conquest is not achieved rationally, by reflection and analysis,
since hope and despair are not of that order and the evidence of
catastrophe too overwhelming. The irrational must be overcome by
some other force, inexplicable and mysterious, a moment of non-
supernatural grace, a small miracle:

> Je n'ai pas encore très bien compris comment cela s'est fait,—en moi et
> en nous. D'ailleurs, je ne cherche pas. Il est de certains miracles très
> naturels. Je veux dire: très faciles à accepter. Je les accepte de grand cœur
> et celui-ci fut de ceux-là. J'y pense souvent. Je m'attendris, je souris et
> m'étire. Je sais qu'il y aurait sûrement quelque chose à trouver. A quoi
> bon? Cette demi- ignorance, ma foi, me convient. (**7**)

The miracle in question is the spectacle of a line of ducklings whose
smallest member struggles against its own weakness and a hostile
environment to keep upright and rejoin the group, an enterprise
whose apparent futility and capacity to inspire compassionate laughter
encourages the downcast men to pick themselves up and face the task
once again. The personal tone of the narrator's introductory
comments, his engaging admission of ignorance, the slight implication
of laziness, and the use of the present tense all invite the reader's
complicity. At the same time, the words 'en moi et en nous' suggest a
collective dimension, announce the dynamics of a story in which
individual silence and withdrawal give way to silence shared, and
thereafter to silence broken by laughter and then by the resolute 'A la
soupe! Venez. Nous en sortirons' (**15**) with which the story closes.
Like the story of Bruce and the spider, *Désespoir est mort* is a
sentimental parable, in some respects more naïve artistically than *Le
Silence de la mer,* and by its publication in 1943 already nostalgic

since the *prise de conscience* it articulates had found concrete expression in the organized Resistance movement. Nonetheless, by virtue of the events and the period described, it was an eminently suitable piece to choose 'en guise de préface' (**5**) to the collection as a whole. Moreover, within his chosen narrative and experiential framework, Vercors offers a detailed and in some ways still mordant critique of historical events and political attitudes.

When the story opens, we find the narrator thrust into a 'mess hétéroclite' with 'une douzaine d'officiers venus de toutes parts, sans point commun sinon celui de n'avoir pas combattu' (**8**). An early observation establishes the representative nature of the circumstances and the singularity of his own feelings: 'Car nous n'étions pas tous désespérés. Oh! non. [...] Chacun était avant tout préoccupé de soi. Et pourvu que tous les chemins ne fussent pas coupés devant lui, prenait le reste assez légèrement' (*ibid.*).

Profiteering, hoarding, and self-indulgence prevail from the commandant downwards. The cook prepares 'des sauces savamment immondes' for their 'repas animés et bruyants' (**11**). Instead of spiritual solace, the young priest 'serves up'—the culinary recall is deliberate—an 'oraison vide et pompeuse' (**13**). In a more telling comment, the narrator explains: 'ce mess était à l'image de ce pays, où seuls les lâches, les malins et les méchants allaient continuer de pérorer; où les autres n'auraient, pour protester, que leur silence' (**9**). Unable to flee to a desert island, the narrator keeps to his quarters—'j'avais choisi ma chambre' (**10**)—thereby equating his apparently negative, physical withdrawal with the more positive adoption of a position: not simply 'garder silence', 'garder la chambre', but 'prendre parti'. Silence is of course a major link with *Le Silence de la mer*, and its characteristic ambivalence—a refuge or a prison?—is also present. The room with its 'mince fenêtre haut placée' is 'un peu comme un cachot' (**10**). 'Prisonnier dans ces murs comme dans les pensées, simples et horribles, que je ne pouvais chasser' (**11**), the narrator evokes 'cet infernal silence, où nous nous étions murés malgré nous'(**10**). The sense of claustration is reinforced by the narrow lanes and single street of the meridional village, 'brûlé de soleil' (**10**) to which they have been confined since the armistice.

The dominant emotion, however, is a sense of disgust. Defeat and its aftermath are likened to 'un abîme fétide', 'une asphyxie immonde' (**7**), a 'honteuse et cruelle comédie' (**9**). Confronted with a 'chef indigne' and the 'preuves immondes et puantes' (**10**) of his companions' self-seeking and vainglorious gratification, the narrator evokes their 'ambition sordide' (*ibid.*), 'la lâcheté de tous' (**11**) and 'la mêlée répugnante des hommes' (**7**), a powerful image which recalls the sub-maritime 'mêlée des bêtes' in *Le Silence de la mer*. His own discomfiture is described as a 'fatal désœuvrement' and a 'torturante

vie'. The apparent disproportion between the ostensible cause of the
narrator's feelings and his portrayal of the moral monstrosity of those
around him, suggest that *Désespoir est mort* continues *Le Silence de
la mer* in more ways than one.

Failure of leadership, combined with a symptomatic desire to
abdicate responsibility to a providential saviour, emerges from
Vercors's use of historical references. In an indirect but unmistakable
critique of Vichy's policy of *attentisme,* the belief that concessions
could be wrested from Germany in exchange for modest sacrifices,
and that France could find her rightful place in the new Europe, we
read that 'en ce juillet-là courait le mythe Laval-Talleyrand: une
canaille, après Waterloo, avait en quelques années refait une France
redoutée; une canaille referait de même. Il suffisait d'attendre' **(8)**.
The same details occur in Vercors's autobiographical account of the
period preceding his demobilisation (**OP**, 203), but the pairing of
Laval and the nineteenth-century diplomat historically associated with
the Napoleonic police chief Fouché—'Vice leaning on the arm of
Crime' in Chateaubriand's celebrated 'infernal vision' of 1815
(*Mémoires d'outre-tombe,* Part Three, Book V)—is an effective
literary device. Other references are more directly contemporary.
The senior officer in the mess is a 'conseiller général du Gard', an
epithet whose ideological possibilities are promptly confirmed by an
early remark to the monarchist captain, Randois:

> 'Randois, vous avez vu? Votre Maurras se range sans restriction derrière
> le Maréchal? [...] Je suis un vieux radical, mais, dans le malheur de la
> patrie, il faut oublier ses convictions'. **(9)**

This profession of faith echoes much-publicised statements of Pétain
himself, while presenting the irony of an appeal for unity lacking
before and still conspicuously absent:

> La plus franche cordialité régnait entre ces hommes galonnés, qui se
> déchiraient l'un l'autre sitôt séparés. Ils étaient tous rivaux, pour une
> raison ou une autre. La débâcle n'avait pas détruit chez eux le goût des
> préséances, dont ils allaient être bientôt privés. **(11)**

More searching is the political condemnation of a newspaper
editorial which another character shows to the narrator:

> ... ce qu'il me fit lire dépassait tout ce qu'on pouvait attendre. Ce que le
> plus grand mépris des hommes n'aurait suffi à nous faire croire sans
> preuve. On nous ressortait, simplement (n'oubliez pas que c'était la
> première fois), Jeanne d'Arc, Sainte-Hélène, et la perfide Albion. Dans
> cette même colonne, sous cette même signature, où trois semaines plus tôt
> le même homme nous parlait encore, avec une délectation sadique, des
> milliers de barbares teutons que la Lys et la Somme charriaient, sanglants
> et putrides, vers la mer. **(12-13)**

Anglophobia, not a new phenomenon in France in 1940, was undeniably exacerbated by Dunkirk (perceived as a British retreat leaving the French to fend for themselves), by Churchill's refusal to commit precious RAF fighter squadrons to the defence of France, and by the Royal Navy's destruction of the fleet at Mers-el-Kebir on 3 July 1940 with the loss of over 1,200 French lives. But the cynical reversal of attitudes which makes the erstwhile ally into the traditional enemy who exiled Bonaparte to Saint Helena and, four centuries earlier than that, burned Joan of Arc, a symbolic figure later exploited by all parties in the conflict, is grimly ironic given the discrepancy between the sanguinary rhetoric used three weeks previously to describe the German losses, and the reality of the battle for France in May-June 1940. This documentary material is used to narrative as well as didactic effect: no-one speaks, the printed page says it all.

Political attitudes are also conveyed by descriptive characterisation:

> Notre pauvre vieux brigand de commandant, conseiller général du Gard, présidait ces joutes, les couvait de ses gros yeux éteints. Il ressemblait, par le visage et l'accent, à un Raimu amolli, à l'un des Fratellini aussi, — celui qui est mort, celui qui cachait ses dérisoires malices sous un aspect de notaire solennel. Il interrogeait l'avenir avec malaise, inquiet de la place qu'il pourrait y creuser pour son adipeuse papelardise. (**8-9**)

As stated, the political attribute here evokes a 'Radical' stereotype, the self-seeking local *notable,* socially conservative but professing 'advanced' opinions, the garrulous Meridional whose verbal jousts changed nothing. The parallels with the lawyer and the actor (Raimu) suggest dissembling and role-playing; mention of the dead clown underlines the tragi-comic impotence and irrelevance suggested in the 'extinguished eyes' and 'derisory' malices; his 'adipeuse papelardise' anticipates the 'fructueuses rapines' in the quartermastery. 'J'aurais dû, moi aussi, haïr cet homme' (**12**), writes the narrator, but he cannot, perhaps because he knows he is slowly dying of uremia. *La Bataille du silence* (p. 68) reveals that this character too had a historical inspiration, Vercors's mess commandant in 1940:

> Commerçant à Montélimar et conseiller général du Gard, ganache radical au long visage gras d'acteur marseillais, dont l'accent mouillé semblait avoir plongé les mots dans son potage: il dévorait comme quatre mais s'endormait quelques secondes entre chaque bouchée, et n'était certainement plus en état de combattre.

But the 'pauvre vieux brigand de commandant' may also owe an indirect, unstated and perhaps unwitting inspiration to a more important historical figure, of whom Vercors wrote that his 'visage défait hantait mon souvenir'(**BS**, 46), the Radical leader in the 1930s and Prime Minister at Munich:

> Vu de près, Daladier me surprit: le fameux 'taureau de Vaucluse' me
> sembla petit, fragile, le visage moins sanguin que rubescent, couperosé,
> sous des yeux ingénus et interrogatifs. Tout en lui respirait l'incertitude,
> voire la timidité, mal cachées sous une expression d'énergie factice, qu'il
> ne parvenait pas d'ailleurs à maintenir continûment. (*ibid.*)

The physical traits presented here correspond only partially to those
of the fictional character, just as the latter only partially replicate
those of the 'conseiller général du Gard'. But the defining ideological
and temperamental characteristics: the extinct volcano; the 'aspect de
notaire solennel'; the references to bastions of provincial Radicalism
(the Gard, the Vaucluse) are common to all three. By calling to mind
Vercors's archetypal 'faux-durs' (**NJ**, 10), *Désespoir est mort* gives
expression to private as well as public ambivalence about the nature of
leadership.

Of Captain Randois, the narrator quickly informs us that 'je ne
l'aimais pas' (**9**), a frank admission of dislike which unlike the
literary-allusive impression created in respect of the Commandant,
presented as 'objective' and hence correct, may be based on a
subjective impression that is amenable to change:

> Dès avant la défaite, tout en lui m'était ennemi: son caractère hautain, ses
> convictions monarchiques, son mépris de la foule. J'évitais de lui parler.
> Je craignais qu'il ne laissât, d'un mot, deviner la satisfaction que les
> malheurs de la République, le triomphe de la tyrannie, devaient avoir fait
> naître en lui. (**8**)

This stereotype of the right-wing monarchist, aristocratic and
disdainful of 'la foule', supposedly delighted by the defeat of the hated
Republic, is an effective piece of characterisation; it also invites the
reader to establish the unstated political credentials of the narrator
who, like his creator Vercors, can be divined to be a republican and a
democrat. Political identification precedes physical description:
Randois's eyes are 'cruels, bleus et froids' (in that order), but his
voice, 'd'une tristesse sans bornes' (**9**), suggests that any satisfaction
derived from the demise of the régime is offset by a greater sense of
loss, a grief which he keeps to himself. Aloof from the self-
gratification around him, he is also cynically lucid about the possible
implications of defeat. 'Les Fridolins?' he notes in response to a
question from the Commandant about German intentions, 'ils nous
auront jusqu'au trognon' (*ibid.*). But since this remark's unstated
conditional—'si l'on n'y fait quelque chose'—might be taken as
inviting resistance and not abject surrender, the man  can be saved for
the fight and is a kindred spirit of the narrator, age, convictions and
temperament notwithstanding: 'il nous rejoignait, [...] nous les
solitaires, nous les muets. [...] Randois nous avait reconnus' (*ibid.*).

The other member of the narrator's musketeer-like trio is also a
veteran of the 'déshonorant simulacre', the intriguingly named

Captain Despérados. Like Randois, his presence provides solace to the narrator:

> J'étais heureux d'avoir Despérados auprès de moi. Je me sentais moins seul. Non pas que nous eussions jamais échangé un mot de quelque importance. Mais, parfois, quand je sentais moi-même se gonfler mon cœur de dégoût, devant chaque nouvelle marque de la funeste insouciance de ces hommes en qui le pays avait cru trouver des chefs, je voyais se tourner vers moi le cou raide, se poser sur moi l'œil dilaté. Nous croisions ainsi nos regards, et cela nous soulageait. Nous n'allions pas plus loin dans nos confidences. (12)

Once again, Vercors reveals that the character had a real-life original, Captain Cabanetos, a man humiliated by events, whose 'visage hautain d'hidalgo que traverse, en diagonale, une longue cicatrice qui lui ouvre l'œil droit comme ferait un monocle, semble avoir pâli d'indignation' (**OP**, 202). Despérados, of whom a retrospective comment confirms that hope must indeed have triumphed over despair—'j'ai presque un effort à faire aujourd'hui pour comprendre, comme je le comprenais alors, qu'un homme pût être si mortellement découragé' (**10**)—is described thus:

> On eût dit qu'il en avait pâli,—pâli à jamais. Il était pâle et raide, raide d'une vieille blessure qui l'empêchait de tourner la tête sans tourner aussi les épaules; et plus pâle d'une cicatrice qui partageait en deux son beau visage de matador grisonnant, ouvrant en passant l'œil droit, comme eût fait un monocle. Et cela lui donnait une expression double, pénétrante et dominatrice. (*ibid.*)

Cabanetos's hidalgo-like features are reproduced in this 'beau visage de matador grisonnant', as are the scar and the monocle. From an observed reality, Vercors has drawn an imaginary protagonist whose ultimate specificity is determined by writerly narrative and didactic purposes. And Despérados owes another trait to his historical model:

> Une seule fois je l'ai entendu rire: quand il a vu *le Petit Dauphinois,* qui la veille encore se léchait les babines des cadavres teutons flottants sur la Somme ou sur l'Aisne, s'en prendre maintenant, tournant casaque avec le vent, à la 'Perfide Albion qui a brûlé Jeanne d'Arc'. Il m'a tendu le journal à travers la table et nous avons ri ensemble à nous déchirer le cœur. (**OP**, 202)

It is this editorial which Despérados shows the narrator. His cynical laughter which breaks the silence and provides a non-verbal form of release anticipating the more positively cathartic, hope-inspiring episode with the ducklings: 'Rarement ai-je assisté à rien d'aussi comique. De sorte que je m'entendis rire, et aussi Despérados, mais non plus de notre affreux rire du matin. Le rire de Despérados était, cette fois, profond et sain et agréable à entendre. Et même le rire un peu sec de Randois n'était pas désagréable' (**15**).

Despérados, it will be noted, is presented in unequivocally favourable terms which set him apart both from Randois, whom the narrator initially dislikes, and from the 'pauvre vieux brigand de commandant': he is a 'real' matador, not a false corsair. His 'vieille blessure [qui] l'empêchait de tourner' (acquired in World War One, presumably), the monocle and his physical stiffness suggest a characterial or intellectual inflexibility strangely reminiscent of the aristocratic German officer von Rauffenstein in Renoir's pacifist *La Grande Illusion* (1937). The similarity is doubtless coincidental— Vercors mentions the film once only (**OP**, 122)—but like other features it strengthens the case for considering such characters as a further literary embodiment of the author's own 'lost illusions', the 'occasions perdues' of the 1930s. And the emphasis given to Despérados's almost definitive pallor ('pâli à jamais') suggests a spectral quality which we have already seen in *Le Silence de la mer*. Like von Ebrennac, he is a 'revenant'; part of him has 'died' in the 'déshonorant simulacre' of battle, of crime and betrayal, of 'murder most foul'. The Shakespearian allusion is deliberate: Vercors spent most of 1943 away from Paris: 'dans ma campagne, j'ignorais tout, travaillais à mon *Hamlet* dans la paix de l'inconscience' (**BS**, 267). Like his condemnation of 'la funeste insouciance' of those from whom the country had expected leadership, this admission reads curiously like a denial.

In fact, the story ends with an admission: 'c'est à ces petits canards délurés, martiaux, attendrissants et ridicules, que je dus, au plus sombre couloir d'un sombre jour, de sentir mon désespoir soudain glisser de mes épaules comme un manteau trop lourd' (**16**). The narrator's emergence from the dark corridor, the evocation of despair sliding from his shoulders like a cape, mark a break with the psychological problematic of the earlier story: Hamlet is no longer in thrall to the obsessive memory of the ghost, the too heavy inheritance of guilt; hope has been regained thanks to a providential intervention and the solidarity of other men, soldier and father-figures whom the narrator can respect the more because he does not have to like them.

The lesson of *Désespoir est mort* is therefore relatively complex. The ducklings call to mind previous struggles against the forces of darkness, 'l'opiniâtreté surhumaine qu'il fallut à quelques moines, au milieu de ces meurtres, de ces pillages, de cette ignorance fanatique, de cette cruauté triomphante, pour se passer de main en main un fragile flambeau pendant près de mille ans' (**15**). And in an echo of *Le Silence de la mer*, the narrator adds: 'Certes, je ne pensai pas précisément tout cela. Mais ce fut comme lorsqu'on voit la reliure d'un livre que l'on connaît bien' (*ibid.*). By the time he came to write *Désespoir est mort*, Vercors himself was the author of just such a book.

In *Désespoir est mort,* silence is a refuge in which isolated individuals recognize their kinship before proclaiming their solidarity. The progression from the non-verbal to the verbal articulates the literary myth of the suffering finding a 'voice', *la parole.* But the story's very existence, with its expressed contempt for eloquence (the perorations of the mess, the cook and the priest), confirms the illustrator and engraver's growing predilection for *l'écriture.*

## L'Imprimerie de Verdun

With *La Marche à l'étoile, L'Imprimerie de Verdun* is the most synoptic of the stories in the collection, since it takes us back to the First World War and extends to the post-Liberation period. But the action centres on the war years, notably the intensification of Vichy's anti-Semitic policies after Laval's return to the premiership in 1942 (*l'étoile jaune,* the deportations). Anti-Vichyssois more than anti-German, it is an appropriate text to study after *Le Silence de la mer* and *Désespoir est mort.*

Vendresse is an 'ancien de Verdun' who inherited his small printing works from his boss and fellow-veteran who died of his wounds. His sole employee, the *Briançonnais* Dacosta, is also a Verdun veteran, who had set up for himself in Piedmont after the war but was forced to leave because of his Jewishness; anti-fascist by conviction as well by racial origin, he is also a Freemason and bears a Communard name. Vendresse dislikes Jews, Communists, and Freemasons... After one of his tirades against these and other 'voleurs' whom he accuses of leading the country to ruin, we read:

> Le commis, juif et franc-maçon, regardait son patron avec une douce ironie... Et Vendresse se sentait un peu bête, fourgonnait ses poches pour y chercher une pipe qu'il savait absente, déplaçait ses petites lunettes rondes sur son petit bout de nez rose, remuait ses grosses lèvres sous la moustache roussie par les mégots. (**114**)

Vendresse is a curious mixture of garrulousness and inarticulacy. This little cameo brings out his rather bumbling naïveté; it also gives him an older quality, which is deceptive—like Dacosta, he is in his forties at the outbreak of hostilities in 1939 (*ibid.* )—and an other-worldliness, which is not. He cannot rationalise—or sees no need to rationalise—the contradiction inherent in his dislike of Jews and Freemasons in general and his affection for Dacosta in particular. Like his workshop cluttered with junk—'vieux clichés, vieilles clefs, vieux cendriers-réclames, vieux écrous et même un vieux manomètre de quelle chaudière?—qu'il ne pouvait se décider à jeter: "ça pourrait servir"' (**112**), his political ideas are an uncritical accumulation of *objets trouvés* and *idées reçues* which find expression in the confidence he continues to place in Pétain: 'Il n'y a que lui pour nous tirer de là' (**115**); 'Tu ne risques rien avec le Vieux' (**116**); 'Laisse Pétain tranquille. Il n'y est pour rien. Ce n'est pas sa faute si des salauds...' (**125**); 'tant que le Vieux sera là' (**128**). This naïveté contrasts with his more clear-sighted employee, in whom political conviction is accompanied by an analytical understanding, however unschooled. But in its humanity, that of a man disinclined to discard the possibly useful, it also contrasts with the chilling expendability preached by the anti-Semitic Paars.

   Vercors uses historical allusion to events of the 1930s to embed character traits and establish the parameters of what will be an ideological critique of the Vichy régime. The railway companies who put profits before safety with outdated wooden rolling stock whose dangers were illustrated in 1933 by the disaster at Lagny, the politico-financial scandals like the Stavisky affair which produced the crisis of 6 February 1934, the social and economic upheavals of the Popular Front and the looming international conflict, all provide abundant scope for arguments—'"ça faillit tourner mal en 36"'—which usually end amicably over a drink, because the two men 's'adoraient' (**113**). Mobilised in 1939 in a non-combatant capacity, they serve in the same unit thanks to the narrator's influence, but with the workplace hierarchies reversed. Vendresse is a mere 'cabot', Dacosta a sergeant who extricates his platoon from the *débâcle* and brings it safely back behind the lines without loss: in this he displays leadership qualities which contrast signally with the example of his superior officers, a captain and two lieutenants who had 'filé' in a Citroën (**115**). This dereliction of duty prompts a dismissive comment from Dacosta, and a rejoinder from Vendresse that they were perhaps acting under orders and that, supreme irony, '"faut pas généraliser"' (*ibid.*), a nice example of his willingness to condone faults in some but not in others.

   But though the effects of this blindness are tragic, his intention is without malice. Like the narrator, whose 'je l'aimais bien' (**111**) is an unmistakable prompt to the reader and whose different political views are an earnest of objectivity—'il m'appelait: "Bolchevik!"'— we warm to Vendresse. His heart in the right place even if his head is not: 'il état fervent et sincère. Sa sincérité, sa ferveur le trompaient de chemin, c'est tout' (*ibid.*). We are obliged to exercise towards him the virtue of tolerance, whose absence—or whose opposite, persecutory intolerance—structures the story.

   Enter the villain of the piece:

> Vers la fin de janvier, Vendresse reçut une visite. C'était un collègue, enfin, un galvano. Sa carte portait: 'Membre de l'Association des Imprimeurs-Graveurs-Brocheurs anciens combattants. Membre de l'Amicale des Vieux de Verdun'. Il s'appelait Paars. (**116**)

'Un collègue, *enfin*, un galvano': well, not quite a colleague, not even an acquaintance. The 'enfin' registers a qualification to which the reader reacts accordingly; distancing is created by the visiting card, which introduces a persona and not a person, gives us detail but not an individual, speaks of self-importance, an economical, almost cinematic touch, unoriginal but effective. Our first impressions are confirmed, and further distancing occurs when we meet Paars face to face: 'Il était gras, un peu trop élégamment vêtu. Ses grosses joues plutôt molles, rasées de près, étaient couperosées sous la poudre' (*ibid.*). The adverbial qualifiers 'plutôt' and 'un peu trop' express a reservation which translates subliminally from the semantic to the moral and intellectual, and thence to the visceral: before Paars has even opened his mouth (but his 'card' has spoken for him) we do not much like this man. Like Balzac, Vercors creates moral revulsion by physical traits; his descriptions are not neutral but designed to elicit an attitude, and, in their use of particular literary/visual conventions (the presence of the cartoonist is tangible here), appear to endorse the otherwise questionable proposition that you can judge by appearances. This impression is further reinforced by what we learn of Paars's war service at Verdun, which belongs to the 'nudge nudge, wink wink' school of combat, in a cushy billet away from the front, 'le filon' (**117**).

Needless to say, the purpose of his visit proves sinister: after a brief exchange about 'la pluie et le beau temps' (**116**), Paars announces that 'c'est le moment de se débarrasser des Juifs dans la profession. On fera une pétition à Vichy. Tu marches avec nous, naturellement?' (**117**). But a further visit reveals a squalid personal motive, too: by removing Dacosta, Paars seeks to place his illegitimate son who is 'un peu en retard pour certaines choses' (**122**) and secure the succession on Vendresse's retirement. This second encounter takes place at the latter's flat, as he is shaving before his weekly visit to the Dacostas for Sunday lunch. Paars's unexpected arrival at his home and not the workplace puts Vendresse at a disadvantage; the shaving, though an unoriginal piece of visual realism, emphasises the invasion of privacy and enables the writer, by a nicely judged piece of indirect speech, to convey Paars's overweening presence: 'Oh! que Vendresse ne se dérange pas, qu'il finisse sa barbe: visite en passant seulement, rien que pour bavarder' (**119**). Like Flaubert;s Monsieur Homais, always arriving at the carefully chosen inopportune moment 'à pas muets pour ne déranger personne' (*Madame Bovary*, Book Two, Chapter IV), and whose 'Bonsoir la compagnie!' simply means that with his own arrival the company is complete, Paars;s opening words say all we need to know about his personality. Once again, descriptive confirmation promptly follows:

Paars cala ses grosses fesses dans le petit fauteuil de cuir, dont le crin
s'échappait un peu d'un côté. Il ne semblait pas très bien savoir où mettre
ses gros bras. Ses bajoues couperosées débordaient le petit col empesé
qu'ornait coquettement un nœud papillon. Il avait des yeux un peu
bizarres, mal plantés dans les paupières, comme ceux d'une limande.
Alors, dit-il en riant, toujours enjuivé?' (**119**)

This passage is an action replay of the previous description of Paars, a
variation on theme and impression: the 'bajoues couperosées', the
physical bulk and flabbiness overflowing his clothes and Vendresse's
dilapidated armchair with the stuffing protruding combine to suggest
the cuckoo in the nest, the parasite. The starchy stiffness of the collar
and the 'coquettish' bow tie suggest a primness powerfully
contradicted by the crude question which announces the true purpose
of the call (emphatically not *bavardage*), while the strange eyes, seen
for the first time, are not quite right, a bit fishy, 'comme ceux d'une
limande'. In common with the self-righteous shopkeeper Poissonnard
of Jean Dutourd's post-war *Au Bon Beurre* (1952), whom he
foreshadows, Paars represents the emergence during the 'National
Revolution' of new profiteers just as corrupt as the old ones. He uses
Pétain's authority and the spurious prestige of the Vichy francisque
emblem for selfish purposes. The vigorous stubbing out of a cigarette
pointedly underlines the veiled threat he utters when Vendresse proves
unamenable to the removal of Dacosta: the mode of address is
appropriately familiar 'entre "Vieux de Verdun"' (**117**), yet clearly
abusive: 'tu sais ce que tu fais, n'est-ce pas?' (**122**).

Vendresse, incapable of marking his distance by linguistic
formality, and trapped within his own contradictions—'les Juifs, c'est
entendu, je les emmerde. Seulement...' (**117**)—is easily worsted by
the cynical Paars, just as he has no convincing answers for the more
clear-sighted Dacosta. He seeks refuge in silence, in reiterated but
increasingly less convincing expressions of trust in Pétain, and finally
lies: Dacosta, he says, is not a Jew (**122**). It is only with the arrest of
another printer, Whemer, betrayed by a Frenchman for defacing his
racial identity card and refusing to wear the yellow Star of David, that
serious doubts assail him. He stops in the street to contemplate
'l'affiche rouge bordée de noir qu'il connaissait bien, la sinistre
affiche où figuraient les noms de dix communistes et autant de Juifs,
fusillés comme otages' (**125**). When Dacosta goes into hiding, we see
Vendresse seated 'sur le marbre, les jambes pendantes, le menton dans
les mains' (**128**), a curious image of childlike vulnerability and
depressive premonition. When, finally, he is unable to prevent the
arrest of Dacosta's family or, through the 'Amicale des Vieux de
Verdun', to secure their release, disillusionment is complete:
'Couillon. Misérable couillon. J'ai cru dans tous ces bandits. Dac
m'avait prévenu' (**131**). Vendresse 'silently' joins the Resistance.

Denounced in his turn, caught with a workshop full of leaflets, tortured in Fresnes prison and then deported himself, he is last heard of in Germany in 1944-1945: 'Maigre à faire peur. Il marchait difficilement. [...] Son corps pitoyable doit reposer quelque part, dans un fossé, au bord d'une route d'Allemagne' (**138**).

Vendresse's fear of 'le projecteur' and his rather matter-of-fact simplicities were borrowed from the jobbing printer Oudeville, who in his small workshop opposite the Pitié hospital printed the first three hundred and fifty copies of *Le Silence de la mer:*

> Je n'ai pas voulu qu'il ignore ce qu'il risque et justement, en face, à l'Hôpital de la Pitié qu'occupent les Allemands, le physicien Holweck agonise. On lui a carbonisé les pieds, arraché les ongles, ouvert le crâne. Oudeville, à son composteur, m'écoute sans s'émouvoir. Une seule torture l'inquiète parce que, l'été, il souffre de conjonctivite: le projecteur puissant qui, braqué nuit et jour, vous détruit la rétine. C'est là une douleur qu'il connaît au soleil. Les autres excèdent son imagination. (**OP**, 234)

As so often in Vercors's writing we find a real-life original for a character. Vendresse retains something of that reality despite his slightly caricatural traits—the uneasy searching for his missing pipe, the embarrassed silences—and his subordination to the writer's didactic purpose. Forging a non-Jewish identity card for Dacosta is Vendresse's first step towards active resistance; is it also a stage in his realization of the hollowness of Vichy's moral values? 'Devenir faussaire, à mon âge', he laments. 'Et dans une France enfin propre. Ça me dégoûte' (**127**). His unthinking, almost automatic attachment to right-wing cliché ('dans une France enfin propre') suggests that the irony of his situation may still escape him: he has been forced to lie in order to protect his workmate from policies introduced by the leader, whose 'portrait en couleurs naturelles' accompanied by the words of one of his speeches—'"Je hais les mensonges"'—adorns the wall of the workshop. It does not escape the narrator, who indulges in some ironical moralising of his own when a chastened Vendresse contacts him about the Resistance: '"Eh bien, c'est du propre! Un vieux fidèle comme vous? Un Pétain-sauvez-la-France, un Maréchal-nous-voilà, un Suivons-le-Chef, un la-France-aux-Français comme vous?"'(**129**). Vendresse will end up fighting for the truth, against the lies and falsehood of the régime associated with the false sovereign, the usurper, evoked in Aragon's memorable couplet: 'Dans l'étrange Paris de Philippe-le-Bel / Le Roi même faisait de la fausse monnaie'.[38]

Vichy is subverted in other ways too. Vendresse may be a 'vieux garçon', but Dacosta has a model family life (and a wife at home, caring for her two young children), he is a good worker and, despite his 'foreign' antecedents, served the *patrie* better than his officers in 1940. His ordinariness is vouchsafed by small details such as the

apéritif taken before Sunday lunch in the little flat in the rue
Froidevaux, 'coquet, propre et ensoleillé' (119) looking out over the
Montparnasse cemetery, and the modest conviviality they share with
Vendresse. Madame Dacosta, we read, 'partageait ses soins entre la
table des grandes personnes et les exigences des bébés' (123). Her 'fin
visage aux lèvres timidement souriantes' and 'yeux noirs intenses et
profonds, toujours un peu humides' touch a protective, 'paternal'
chord in Vendresse which reinforces his subsequent guilt. The
reassuring 'normality' of their lives is retrospectively confirmed by
the information that the workshop has been taken over 'par un vieux
typo en retraite, pourri d'alcool' and 'un apprenti étrange, un
adolescent à la tête trop grosse, sauvage et silencieux, sujet à de
brusques colères qui impressionnent le voisinage' (138). The
deportation of Dacosta's family, like the imposition of the *Service du
Travail Obligatoire* in February 1943, is a powerful indictment of
Vichy's collaboration, an indictment more graphically expressed on
walls and public places by the Resistance's alteration of the slogan
'Travail, Famille Patrie' to 'Travail forcé, famille brisée, patrie
vendue!' and 'Tracasseries, famine, patrouilles!'

  *L'Imprimerie de Verdun* is in some ways Vercors's most bitter and
most uncompromising story. The moral cards are stacked
unashamedly in favour of the heroes, and yet corruption triumphs
over virtue. When the story appeared in August 1945, it already
contained an embryonic critique of the post-Liberation order: Paars
has been playing a double game on behalf of the Resistance, he enjoys
the favour of the authorities, and is clearly destined for high position
in the new régime: 'il est très au courant de toutes les questions
concernant l'électrolytique. Il serait, dit-on, difficile de se passer de
lui. C'est un gros bonnet dans l'Office de Répartition. Il y fait la pluie
et le beau temps' (139). Just like Homais after the demise of Emma
and Charles, of whom we read in the closing lines of Madame Bovary
that: 'Il fait une clientéle d'enfer; l'autorité le ménage et l'opinion
publique le protège. Il vient de recevoir la croix d'honneur'.

## L'Impuissance

Vendresse and Dacosta, his wife and children are emblematic of the
martyrdom of humble, unsung heroes, whose poetry was in the
texture of their daily lives. The martyrdom of the writer and critic
Benjamin Crémieux in Buchenwald was the the pretext for, if not the
inspiration of, *L'Impuissance,* written in July 1944. Its impetuous,
rebellious hero, Renaud, 'toujours prêt à payer lui-même pour les
péchés du monde' (90), is a boyhood friend of the narrator who, as in

*L'Imprimerie de Verdun,* influences our attitude towards characters. They are presented as different but, because of his respect, admiration or indulgence, worthy of our own. The introductory admission that 'je le connais depuis si longtemps qu'il m'est difficile d'imaginer une part de ma vie sans lui' (**89**) indeed invites the supposition that the protagonist is a projection of the author-narrator. This normalising function is reinforced by a literary cliché, the evocation of Renaud's arrival in the narrator's class at school; the clumsy and indistinct 'Rémoulade' he utters when asked his name (Renaud Houlade) by the teacher echoes the 'Charbovari' proferred by Flaubert's more famous 'nouveau' in the opening chapter of *Madame Bovary.* His loyalty and visceral need to share in the injustice dealt to others are established on that first encounter, when he is excluded from class for his refusal to betray a fellow-pupil. Four years of Nazi occupation, 'ces quatre ans que la France a passés au fond des catacombes' (**90**), have produced further evidence of these qualities, as the narrator reports:

> Ce n'est pas une fois, mais dix, qu'il m'a fallu l'empêcher de commettre quelque irrémédiable sottise. Il voulut arborer l'étoile jaune, se porter otage volontaire. Il finit par comprendre la vanité de ces révoltes. D'autres ont souffert, ont maigri de faim. Lui maigrissait, se consumait de rage rentrée. Inutile de vous dire qu'il se lança dans la résistance à corps perdu. C'est un miracle qu'il soit encore en vie. (**90-91**)

No details are given of Renaud's Resistance activities, but his 'rage rentrée' and frustrated desire for action set the stage for the catalytic event, the news of the death of Bernard Meyer, 'en Silésie, dans son camp [...]. D'extrême faiblesse' (**92**), a phrase which conjures up the previously-quoted lines (*supra,* p. 40) from Act One, Scene V of *Hamlet* (**93**). The recourse to a literary reference of predilection is Vercors's way of naming the unnamable and of admitting that mere words will not suffice. But the framing of the quotation between a shared but unstated vision of the dead man—'je sus que l'image de Bernard Meyer flottait entre nous'—and the evocation of Renaud's silent 'regard de pierre'(*ibid.*) actualises the 'ghostly' sub-text common to several of the stories and gives Renaud's and the narrator's 'étrange combat' (*ibid.*) greater resonance.

For their sentiments are coloured by the uneasy knowledge that Meyer 'avait, à tous et à chacun, rendu plus de services que quiconque sur terre. Avait-on fait (ceux qui l'auraient pu) tout le possible pour le tirer de Drancy? Nous savions bien, Renaud et moi, que non. Et nous savions bien pourquoi,—et ce n'était pas reluisant' (**92**). This solidarity in unspoken guilt is temporarily displaced but not definitively dispelled by Renaud's predictably explosive reaction: he makes a bonfire of the books and paintings in his library, and prepares to incinerate the iconic objects of Western humanist culture, the lies which had not prevented the horrors of Nazism. Yet however predictable, the violence of this behaviour troubles the narrator, who suspects that 'quelque élément m'était caché' (**91**), and who realizes instinctively that his friend risks being no better than the Nazi book-burners, and of being wrong: without art and literature there is no refuge from the horror, no antidote to it, no permanent repository of values. The still-present memory of 'les longues minutes de lourd silence qui passèrent alors, je ne les oublierai plus' (**93**), leads into a conventionally stylised evocation of the scene in terms which prefigure Renaud's own failure to understand: 'il faisait chaud, les volets étaient fermés aux trois quarts pour sauver ce qui se pouvait d'une fraîcheur mourante... Un insecte—guêpe ou bourdon—se cognait sans cesse au vasistas avec l'entêtement absurde d'une fatale incompréhension' (*ibid.*). Called upon yet again to deflect Renaud from 'quelque irrémédiable sottise', but acutely aware that mere reason will not suffice, the narrator himself is virtually powerless until the pent-up emotion underlying Renaud's increasingly strident indictment has run its course, and the latter, 'tapant du pied, comme un enfant coléreux que le chagrin met hors de lui' (**98**), lashing out left and right indiscriminately, finally succumbs to violent, grief-stricken sobbing. Renaud's crisis is more regressive than von Ebrennac's but ultimately perhaps, equally cathartic.

The themes of *L'Impuissance* are those of *Le Silence de la mer* (the cultural problematic) and *L'Imprimerie de Verdun* (*la fausse parole*, Resistance and the holocaust). Unlike von Ebrennac, however, it is a French protagonist who is in danger of losing faith in his civilisation:

> Et tu voudrais que je garde tout ça sur mes rayons? Pour quoi faire? Pour, le soir, converser élégamment avec Monsieur Stendhal, comme jadis, avec Monsieur Baudelaire, avec Messieurs Gide et Valéry, pendant qu'on rôtit tout vifs des femmes et des gosses dans une église? Pendant qu'on massacre et qu'on assassine sur toute la surface de la terre? Pendant qu'on décapite des femmes à la hache? Pendant qu'on entasse les gens dans des chambres délibérément construites pour les asphyxier? Pendant qu'un peu partout des pendus se balancent aux arbres, aux sons de la radio qui donne peut-être bien du Mozart? (**97-8**)

This impassioned outburst is in a way a critique of *Le Silence de la mer*, too unsubversive of its own codes and values. It also marks a further step in the grim descent into the darkness of civilisation, the horror represented not just by Bernard Meyer (Crémieux), but by other martyrs: the poet Max Jacob, who died of pulmonary congestion at Drancy in February 1944, en route to Germany, Robert Desnos, of typhus at Teresina in April 1945, and not just by individual cases, which the story transcends, but by other atrocities nearer home. The 'hidden element' as yet unknown to the narrator is revealed by Renaud's reference to the women and children burned alive in a church: four days after the D-Day landings, the mass murder

committed at Oradour-sur-Glane by the SS 'Das Reich' Division on 10
June 1944 epitomized the horror of which Nazism would remain
capable until the very end.

Clearly, we have come a long way from the uplifting message of
the ducklings that signalled the 'death of despair' and the willingness
to *passer le flambeau* that would ensure the permanence of French
cultural tradition. The narrator finally concludes affirmatively:
'Pensé-je comme Renaud? Non pas, tout au contraire! L'art seul
m'empêche de désespérer. L'art donne tort à Renaud. Nous le voyons
bien que l'homme est décidément une assez sale bête. Heureusement
l'art, la pensée désintéressée le rachètent' (**99**). But as in *Le Silence
de la mer* and *L'Imprimerie de Verdun,* there is ambivalence, the
recognition that things can never be as they were: 'Et pourtant, depuis
ce jour, j'ai perdu la joie de lire' (*ibid.*). Like the Pyrrhic victor von
Ebrennac, the narrator recognizes both the futility of words, read or
said, and yet their ultimate necessity. And like Vendresse, his
sentiments are due in part to his own 'mauvaise conscience' (**100**).
Why? he had not fought enough for his beliefs, he had accepted the
comforting justifications of art and literature: 'Devant mes tableaux,
devant mes livres, je détourne un peu les yeux. Comme un filou, pas
encore endurci, qui ne peut jouir avec un cœur tranquille de ses
trésors dérobés' (*ibid.*). His uneasy conclusion raises familiar
questions about the role of the artist and intellectual in human affairs,
questions also addressed to the invisible interlocutor present in all the
stories, the Baudelairean 'hypocrite lecteur, mon semblable, mon
frère'.

# Conclusion

Jean Bruller can scarcely have foreseen in 1940 that four years later, the mountain plateau from which he took his pseudonym would be the scene of bitter combat between Resistance and German and Vichy forces, and that in more peaceful times it would become a 'parc naturel régional'. Nor can he have foreseen the celebrity which would be enjoyed by *Le Silence de la mer*, in its own way just as important a part of the Resistance struggle as the 'combats du Vercors'. Its undeniable historic significance does not however suffice to make Vercors's wartime writing 'great literature' in the way in which the phrase is habitually understood. Stories about the Holocaust and the camps such as *Le Songe* and *L'Impuissance* display few of the evocative powers of post-war works by Élie Wiesel or Jorge Semprun. The narrative and descriptive talents deployed in *Désespoir est mort*, *L'Imprimerie de Verdun* and *La Marche à l'étoile* are slight compared with those of Jean-Louis Curtis or André Schwarz-Bart. But Vercors himself did not experience 'l'univers concentrationnaire' at first hand, nor was detailed social chronicle his intention; mention of these post-war novelists situates Vercors in a literary landscape, giving an order of magnitude rather than a measure of achievement, and fairer comparisons would be with the short stories of Claude Aveline, Jean Dutourd or Elsa Triolet. *Le Silence de la mer* itself, his most 'canonical' text, has never belonged to that category represented by Alain-Fournier's *Le Grand Meaulnes*, described by an earlier commentator (Paul Nizan?) as a famous work which no-one had the courage to dislike. But if not a great work, and even though a highly derivative one which continues to have detractors as well as admirers, it remains unique and individual. Scheler's analogy with the Statue of Liberty (*supra*, p. 1) appropriately but unwittingly preserves some of the symbolic ambiguities of an original that was exported to the Anglo-Saxon world by France, inextricably linked to and mythicised with a Resistance consciousness which since 1945 has been part of the French national identity, before becoming part of the way we think about literature itself.

Vercors

# 'Le Silence de la mer' et autres récits

A critical introduction to the wartime writing

William Kidd

in French,
ty of Stirling

LIVERPOOL
UNIVERSITY
LIBRARY

For cond

UNIVERSITY OF GLASGOW FRENCH & GERMAN PUBLICATIONS 1991

University of Glasgow French and German Publications

Series Editors:   Mark G. Ward (German)
Geoff Woollen (French)

Consultant Editors :  Colin Smethurst
Kenneth Varty

Modern Languages Building, University of Glasgow,
Glasgow G12 8QL, Scotland.

First published 1991; reprinted 1991.

Printed by Castle Cary Press, Somerset BA7 7AN.

**ISBN**    **0 85261 316 4**